Further Ahead

A communication skills course
for Business English

Learner's Book

Sarah Jones-Macziola
with Greg White

CAMBRIDGE
UNIVERSITY PRESS

PUBLISHED BY THE PRESS SYNDICATE OF THE UNIVERSITY OF CAMBRIDGE
The Pitt Building, Trumpington Street, Cambridge CB2 1RP, United Kingdom

CAMBRIDGE UNIVERSITY PRESS
The Edinburgh Building, Cambridge CB2 2RU, UK
40 West 20th Street, New York, NY 10011–4211, USA
477 Williamstown Road, Port Melbourne, VIC 3207, Australia
Ruiz de Alarcón 13, 28014 Madrid, Spain
Dock House, The Waterfront, Cape Town 8001, South Africa

http://www.cambridge.org

First published 2003

Printed in Italy by G Canale & C. S.p.A

A catalogue record for this book is available from the British Library

Library of Congress Cataloguing in Publication data

ISBN 0 521 53172 1 Learner's Book
ISBN 0 521 59785 4 Learner's Book Cassette
ISBN 0 521 63928 X Learner's Book CD
ISBN 0 521 59784 6 Teacher's Guide
ISBN 0 521 59783 8 Home Study Book
ISBN 0 521 59782 X Home Study Cassette
ISBN 0 521 63929 8 Home Study CD
ISBN 0 521 58779 4 Video and Teacher's Guide (VHS PAL)
ISBN 0 521 58778 6 Video and Teacher's Guide (VHS SECAM)
ISBN 0 521 58777 8 Video and Teacher's Guide (VHS NTSC)
ISBN 0 521 62645 5 Video Activity Book

Contents

1 People

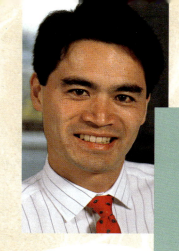

1.1 Meeting people

A Look at these pictures. Where are the people? Do they know each other?

a

b

c

B 📼 ◎ Now listen to three conversations. Match them to the correct picture.

C Study these introductions and greetings.

Introducing yourself

Hello, | I'm *Gina*.
| my name's *Paulo*.

A: How do you do?
Pleased to meet you.
B: How do you do?
Pleased to meet you, too.

Introducing someone else

This is *Wendy*.
I'd like to introduce *Dirk*.

Do you know *Mikiko*?
Have you met *Oscar*?

Greeting someone you know

A: How are you?
B: Fine thanks.
Not too bad, thank you.

Look at the pictures in **A** again and practise the conversations with a partner. Talk about yourself this time.

D Find out about other learners. Use this table to help you.

	Learner 1	Learner 2	Learner 3	Learner 4
Name				
Country				
Profession				
Company				

Now introduce two of these people to the rest of the class like this:

This is (name).
S/he's from (country).
S/he's a/n (occupation).
S/he works for (company).

A A visitor is coming to your company. You are meeting them for the first time. Write down three questions you can ask.

1

2

3

B Listen to Bruno Soares talking to Ms Novak, a visitor to his company in Porto, Portugal. Are his questions the same as yours?

Listen again and write down the questions you think help to keep the conversation going.

C Practise the questions with a partner. Use your own information for the answers.

D Look at these questions. Match them to a picture.

1 Where are you staying? ☐
2 Is the traffic always like this? ☐
3 What do you think of the conference? ☐
4 Do you work here in Paris? ☐
5 Is it your first trip to New York? ☐
6 Did you have a good flight? ☐

a

b

c

d

e

f

Which ones does the host (H) ask, which ones does the visitor (V) ask and which ones could either (E) ask?

Think of an answer to each question. Then choose one of the situations and prepare a dialogue.

A What do you think this subscription form is for:

A book club?   A CD club?   A magazine?

SAVE 20% ON THE NEWSSTAND PRICE
You pay only AUD$4.96 per issue instead of AUD$6.20

Please write in BLOCK CAPITALS

Surname: ....

First name: ....

Job title: ....

Company name: ....

Address: ....

City: ....

Country: ....

Tel.: .... Fax: ....

I wish to pay by:

Cheque ☐   Mastercard ☐   Visa ☐

Credit card ☐   American Express ☐

Account number ....

Valid until ....

Signature ....

Now try to complete the form for Pamela Thomas.

PAMELA THOMAS

EXTRATOUR

300 Bourke Street,
Melbourne 3000

Tel. (61 3) 9672 6500
Fax (61 3) 9605 3002

B 🔲 ◎ Listen to the subscription office calling Pamela Thomas and fill in any missing information.

C Study these ways of checking information.

> Your first name**'s** Pamela, **isn't it?**
> You**'re** an accountant, **aren't you?**
> You work for Extratour, **don't you?**

Now check information about Simon Tan like this:

1 Your name's Simon Tan, *isn't it?* ....
2 You work for McCash, ...
3 You're the Assistant Manager, ...
4 You live in Portland, ...
5 You're American, ...
6 You're not married, ...

McCash

41 Second Avenue
Portland, OR 97712

Simon Tan   Tel. (503) 767 1111
Assistant Manager Fax (503) 767 1212

Write down some things you know about other learners in the class and then check your information with them.

D Practise checking information about other people. Learner A looks at File 1 on page 117 and Learner B looks at File 2 on page 120.

2 Talking about companies

AIMS

Describe different types of companies
Find out about companies
Find out about a particular product

Past time
Past simple – statements and questions

Irregular verbs

Questions
Who, What, etc.

2.1 Describing a company

A Look at these company names and logos. What lines of business do you think they are in? Use the industries in the box below to help you.

Aerospace   Airline   Banking   Bar coding   Catering   Computing
Financial services   Food processing   Packaging   Telecommunications   Transport
Vehicle manufacturing

B Compare your answers in small groups like this:

I think Jupiter Sciences could be in the airline business.

I don't agree. I think it's in aerospace.

I agree with you. I'm sure it's in aerospace.

C Now match these company profiles to the companies in **A.**

1 ....

We are a space technology company that designs, manufactures and markets a broad range of space products and services, including spacecraft systems, satellite-based data computation and observation services.

2 ....

We opened our first restaurant in 1978 and currently operate the largest chain in the country with 103 restaurants.

Our restaurants feature best quality Tex-Mex food and traditional-style Mexican food at affordable prices. We provide an alternative to higher-priced traditional sit-down restaurants and lower quality fast food establishments.

3 ....

We manufacture and market a range of consumer packaging in metal, glass and plastics. Our main customers are in the European beverage and food industries. We are one of the leading packaging companies in Europe with production units in Sweden, Denmark, Norway, the Netherlands, Germany, the UK and Austria. We have approximately 5,300 employees, 75% of whom work outside Sweden.

4 ....

We are a Russian-based brokerage and consulting company established in 1992 at the start of the privatization process in Russia. Our main office is located in Moscow and we also have regional branches in Siberia and the Krasnodar region. We deal in shares of Russian privatized enterprises and also provide a full range of financial services related to Russian securities operations.

D You are doing some research on this company. How many of these questions can you answer from this text?

1 What's the name of your company?
2 What line of business are you in?
3 What goods or services does your company provide?
4 How many employees does your company have?
5 Where are your headquarters?
6 Where are your main markets?

▭ ◎ Listen and check your answers. Then practise asking and answering these questions with a partner.

The long-term goal of the Atlas Copco Group is to be the world's leading company within its specialized areas of business: compressor, construction and mining and industrial technologies. The group employs more than 21,000 people, of whom 14% work outside Sweden. Operations are conducted through 17 divisions, which manufacture products in 57 plants in 15 countries. The major share of manufacturing is conducted within European Union countries. Each division has total business responsibility.

E Find out about another learner's company. Then report back to the rest of the group like this:

... works for ... company.
They're in the ... business. They make ...
They have ... employees
The headquarters are in ...
Their main markets are ...

A Read this article. What kind of business is Servcorp?

Instant office
at the ready

For the first six weeks Joan Slater sat alone in an empty office. 'I thought I had a good idea, but then I wasn't so sure', she remembers.

In 1978 she set up her company, called it Servcorp and leased half a floor of a central Sydney building. Her business plan was to meet the temporary office needs of busy business people. In those first six weeks she was general manager and the only employee of the company! However things got better when an overseas lawyer became her first client. Servcorp's secretaries, receptionists and other employees have been busy ever since.

Today Slater runs a network throughout Australia and Southeast Asia. Servcorp now leases a total of 22 floors of office space. The company offers modern office facilities complete with staff, telecommunication links and computers. As a business takes its first steps offshore, it has to have somewhere to call home. Servcorp's offices in Singapore, Malaysia and Thailand and in ten Australian cities provide these homes.

Annual turnover was US$28 million last financial year and the company made a large profit. Servcorp is now expanding in Japan, Korea and China. Slater went to Japan last June where she studied Japanese and established Servcorp offices in Tokyo and Osaka. She said the secret was to set up the business to an international standard. 'Our client can expect the same quality of service as they move from country to country.'

Now correct these statements.

1 Slater started her business in Melbourne.
2 Servcorp was a success from the start.
3 The first client was a local lawyer.
4 Servcorp provides offices, but not staff for new businesses.
5 Servcorp operates in Australia, Southeast Asia, Japan and the USA.
6 The company's turnover was AUD$28m last year.

B Match a word or phrase in the text with these definitions.

a to start a new company
b a report saying what your company aims to do
c something that lasts for a short time
d equipment or services for a particular purpose
e to get bigger

C Study the past simple tense.

Statements

She | **called** the company Servcorp.
      | **leased** a building in Sydney.

Questions

What **did** she **call** her company?
Where **did** she **go** last year?

These verbs are irregular. Find them in the article and write the past simple next to the base form.

be	....	have	....	make	....
become	....	get	....	say	....
do	*did*	go	....	think	....

Here are the answers to some questions. What are the questions? Use the words in the box to help you.

When (x2)   Where   Who   What   Why

1 In 1978. *When did Joan Slater set up her business?* ....
2 In the centre of Sydney. ....
3 An overseas lawyer. ....
4 US$28 billion. ....
5 To set up an office. ....
6 June, last year. ....

D Work with a partner. One learner takes the role of Joan Slater and the other the interviewer. Add three more questions of your own and interview your partner.

2.3 Getting product information

A You work for ABC Computing in Taipei. You receive a letter from X Electronics in Mexico. Where do these parts of the letter go?

1 Truly yours
   M. A. Park
   M. A. Park (Ms)
   Sales Manager

2 May 21, 199–

3 Dear Sir or Madam:

4 ABC Computing
   F8, no 142, Min-Chuan E. Rd
   Sec. 3 Taipei
   Taiwan

5 X Electronics
   Jaie Balmes 11
   COL Los Morales
   11510 Mexico D.F.
   Mexico

I saw your advertisement in this month's issue of
Asia-Pacific Computing World and would like to receive
more information on your range of electronic components.

I look forward to hearing from you.

B Now write a reply to X Electronics in Mexico.

Here are some phrases you can use. Can you complete them?

Thank you for your letter of ....
We enclose ....
Please contact me if ....

C 📼 ◎ This is Rita Tong. She is a colleague of yours at ABC Computing. Her job is to answer enquiries and send out information to customers.

Listen to her taking some calls and complete the addresses:

Paul ....
AFC
.... West Capitol Street
....
Arkansas ....

Erica ....
TAZ Technologies
.... Street
San Francisco
California ....

D Rita Tong is off sick today and you are taking calls for her. Practise this conversation with a partner.

Answer the phone.

Ask for information about *Vari-X* filters.

Offer to send brochures.
Ask for caller's name and address.

Give your name and address.

Promise to mail information today.

Finish the call.

E Practise dealing with enquiries on the phone. Learner A looks at File 3 on page 124 and Learner B looks at File 4 on page 120.

AIMS

Talk about company organization
Draft an advertisement for a vacancy
Talk about your job and its responsibilities
Ask to speak to someone and to leave a message

Present time
Present simple and present progressive

3 Jobs

3.1 Company structure

A Look at this organigram of Comex Xpress. Put the departments in the correct box.

Finance   Human Resources   Production   Sales/Marketing

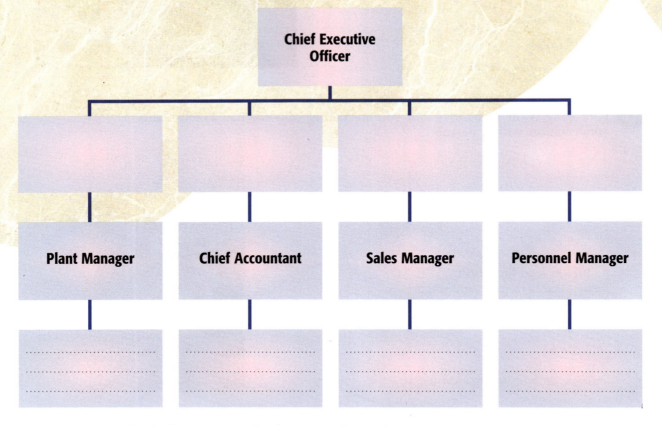

Chief Executive Officer

Plant Manager | Chief Accountant | Sales Manager | Personnel Manager

Which departments do these people work in?

Accounts Clerk	Credit Controller	Maintenance Officer
After-sales Clerk	Quality Controller	Purchasing Officer
Pay Clerk	Sales Representative	Recruitment Officer
Export Clerk	Technician	Training Officer

B 📼 ◎ Now listen to the training officer of Comex Xpress explaining the company structure to some new employees. Check your answers in **A**.

C Look at these two job advertisements. What positions do you think they are for?

We are a successful advertising agency located in the central business district. We are looking for someone with good keyboard skills. A pleasant telephone manner and the ability to deal with clients are also essential. We can offer the successful applicant an attractive salary and a pleasant work environment.

Our firm is one of the leading importers of engineering tools with offices close to the city centre.

We are seeking a person who can sell and is willing to travel. A clean driving licence is essential.

We are offering an attractive salary and benefits package including six weeks' holiday a year.

For an application form or further information, please ring 01225 334455.

D You need an assistant at work. Make notes about the job under these headings and then draft an advertisement for this person.

Your company

Skills and qualifications

Working conditions

3.2 Describing responsibilities

A These people all work for Acme International. What department do you think each person works in?

I'm responsible for invoicing our customers.

I'm in charge of the training programme.

I deal with customer problems.

I deal with enquiries about our products.

I'm responsible for buying raw materials.

I'm in charge of software development.

B Now listen to interviews with them and complete the chart.

Speaker	Department	Current projects
Frank		sending reminders to slow payers
Suzanne		
Peter	Technical Services	
Uschi		
Rolando		
Elke		

C Study the present tenses.

Present simple (usually, often, sometimes) I **send** out invoices to customers. He **organizes** conferences. We **deal** with customer complaints.	**Present progressive** (around now, temporarily) I**'m sending** reminders to slow payers. He**'s organizing** the sales conference. We**'re preparing** for a trade fair.

Now make some sentences about the people at Acme International like this:

Frank works in Accounts. He sends out invoices to customers.
At the moment he's sending reminders to slow payers.

Then practise asking and answering with a partner.

D Make a list of your responsibilities. Then make notes on what you are doing at the moment.

> I work in the *Accounts* department.
>
> I'm | responsible for *invoicing our customers*.
> | in charge of *sending out invoices*.
>
> I deal with *invoices and payments*.
>
> At the moment I'm *sending out reminders*.

Find out about another learner. Use these questions to help you:

What do you do?
What are your responsibilities?
Do you have to ...?
What are you doing at the moment?

3.3 Leaving a message

A 🔊 ◎ Look at these two messages. Which department do you think each person works in?

**GIZMO GADGETS
MESSAGE**

For: Stephanie Crooke
From: Hugh Paine

Please send the list of last month's payments to head office by Friday, 13th.

**GIZMO GADGETS
MESSAGE**

For: Stephen Stern
From: Tanya Cordrey

Please call about order no. 3574 tomorrow before 9 a.m. on 293 554.

Now listen to the phone calls. <u>Underline</u> any mistakes in the messages.

B 🔊 ◎ Listen to another phone call. This time you should write down the message.

**GIZMO GADGETS
MESSAGE**

For:
From:

C Study these expressions. They are often used on the phone.

Asking to speak to someone

I'd like to speak to *Stephanie*.
Could you put me through to *Rolando*?

Saying someone is not available

I'm afraid | she's in a meeting.
he's on holiday.
the line's engaged.
there's no reply.

Asking to leave a message

Could I leave a message?
Could you take a message?

THE FAR SIDE By GARY LARSON

Well, I'm out in the southwest field right now, but I should be home in about an hour.

The rural professional and his cowphone

Now practise this phone call with a partner.

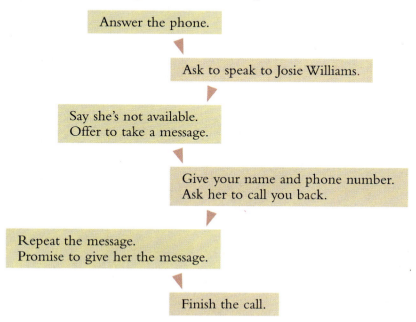

Answer the phone.

Ask to speak to Josie Williams.

Say she's not available.
Offer to take a message.

Give your name and phone number.
Ask her to call you back.

Repeat the message.
Promise to give her the message.

Finish the call.

D Practise taking messages. Learner A looks at File 7 on page 118 and Learner B looks at File 8 on page 123.

AIMS

Make and accept/reject invitations
Talk about hobbies and interests
Get information
Talk about likes and dislikes

Verb patterns
Verbs followed by *-ing*

Adverbs of frequency

4 Work and play

4.1 Inviting

A You're in Sydney on business. What would you like to do in your free time?

B 🔲 ◎ Malcolm Carey is an Australian businessman and often entertains clients who visit his company in Sydney. Listen to three conversations with a client. What does he invite her to do?

	Invitation	Reply (✔/✗)
1		
2		
3		

Listen again. Does she accept (✔) or decline (✗) the invitations?

C Study these ways of making, accepting and declining invitations.

Inviting

Would you like to *have dinner with me tonight*?
How about *taking a harbour cruise*?

Accepting

I'd love to.
That sounds nice.
That would be great.

Declining

I'm afraid | I'm leaving tomorrow.
I'm visiting a client.
I have a meeting.

Now practise making invitations with a partner like this.

Make an invitation.

Decline. Give a reason.

Make an alternative invitation.

Accept.

D Practise making more invitations. Learner A looks at File 11 on page 116 and Learner B looks at File 12 on page 121.

4.2 Getting to know you

A Look at what these people say. Who do you agree with?

Once a relationship of trust has been established, the moment is right for business.

I like to get down to business immediately. If all goes well, I may socialize afterwards.

B How can you get to know a business partner better? Identify possible topics of conversation in the illustration below. Where and when can you talk about these things?

C 🔲 ◎ Listen to two people talking at dinner. Who does what?

Activity	Man	Woman
Mountain biking		
Gardening		
Jogging		
Sailing		
Cinema		
Reading		

D Study these ways of talking about your interests and hobbies.

Work with a partner. Find five things you have in common. You can ask questions like this:

What do you do in your free time?
Do you play any sports?
Do you ever ...?
Do you like ...?
Are you interested in ...?

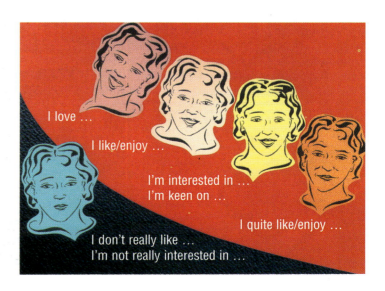

I love ...

I like/enjoy ...

I'm interested in ...
I'm keen on ...

I quite like/enjoy ...

I don't really like ...
I'm not really interested in ...

A You work for a market research company. What kind of products do you think these people would be interested in? Match each one to a product below.

B Look at this questionnaire. Which of the products in **A** do you think the company is researching? Do you think the person answering the questions would be interested in it?

Age: 15–18 19–24 (25–34) 35–49 50–64 65+ **Sex:** (M)/F	1	2	3	4	5	6
Travels for business			✗			
Works at home						✗
Gives presentations					✗	
Does own typing						✗
Uses computer at work			✗			
Buys computer magazines					✗	
(1 = regularly; 2 = frequently; 3 = often; 4 = sometimes; 5 = seldom; 6 = never)						

C ▭ ◎ Listen to an interview with another potential customer for the same product and complete the questionnaire. Do you think she would be interested in the product?

Age: 15–18 19–24 25–34 35–49 50–64 65+ **Sex:** M/F	1	2	3	4	5	6
Travels for business						
Works at home						
Gives presentations						
Does own typing						
Uses computer at work						
Buys computer magazines						
(1 = regularly; 2 = frequently; 3 = often; 4 = sometimes; 5 = seldom; 6 = never)						

D Work with a partner. Choose one of the products in **A** and prepare a market research questionnaire for it.

You can use questions like this:

Do you ever …?
How often do you …?
When did you last …?
What kind of …?
Do you prefer …?
How much do you spend on …?

When you have prepared it, interview some other learners. Are they potential customers?

5 Revision and consolidation

A **Grammar** Correct the mistakes in these sentences.

a Joachim is engineer.
b He work in the Frankfurt office.
c You work for IBM, doesn't you.
d Had you a good journey?
e I start working at this company when I left school.
f When joined you the company?
g Did you went to last year's sales conference?
h Anita works in After-sales – she's dealing with customer complaints.
i We develop a new model at the moment.
j Would you like seeing the factory after lunch?
k Are you interesting in sports?
l I play often tennis and I sometimes play golf.

B **What do you say?** Match the function to the actual words.

1 Introduce a colleague.
2 Ask for information about a product.
3 Ask who someone works for.
4 Invite someone to do something.
5 Offer to take a message.
6 Say what you do.
7 Ask someone about their interests.
8 Ask to speak to someone on the phone.

a Can I give him a message?
b I'm responsible for enquiries about our products.
c Have you met Ms Suzuki?
d Do you play any sports?
e Who do you work for?
f Could I speak to someone in Accounts, please?
g How about a drink after the meeting?
h Could you send me some information on your filter systems?

Now write a short dialogue using some of these phrases.

C **Vocabulary** Look at these categories. How many words can you put in each category?

Departments   Lines of business   Professions

D **Reading** Read this article about Reuben Singh. Why is he unusual?

Another million made, then back in time for school
by Geoffrey Beattie

Reuben Singh is 18 and studying for his final exams at William Hulme School, Manchester. He also runs his own business, Reuben Singh Holdings, which deals in fashion jewellery and accessories. He is worth almost £10m.

The recipe for his success is simple: 'Girls don't have the money to go out and buy new clothes every day. By using accessories they can change how their clothes look. It's also a business with a good turnover and a very high profit margin.'

He started learning about business at the age of 12 in his parents' company, which supplies fashion jewellery to British chain stores. He began by dealing with customers. Then he started to accompany his mother on buying trips to the Far East. At 14 he made his first independent trip – accompanied by 12

The Independent Craig Easton (freelance)

assistants. He dealt directly with the manufacturers and negotiated with chain stores. Four years later, at 18, he says he is almost a veteran businessman. He makes nine or ten trips a year to the Far East, and travels to Milan and Barcelona nearly every week.

The Independent on Sunday 21 May 1995

E **Listening** Listen to an interview with a young businesswoman and take notes on what she does at these times:

5.00	....
7.00	....
8.45	....
12.30	....
15.30	....
21.00	....
24.00	....

Make notes on your day and tell a partner about it.

Summary

Question tags

Positive sentences	Negative sentences
Pamela **is** an accountant, **isn't she**?	She**'s not** married, **is she**?
She **works** for Extratour, **doesn't she**?	She **doesn't** smoke, **does she**?

Present simple tense

I **work** in After-sales.
We **don't export** to South America.
Do you **deal** with customer complaints? Yes, I **do**.

Use To talk about activities which happen again and again or all the time.
N.B. We often use adverbs of frequency with the present simple.

Adverbs of frequency

always   regularly   often   sometimes   seldom   never   frequently

N.B. Adverbs of frequency go before the main verb but after the verb *to be*.

Present progressive tense

I**'m working** on the sales report.
We**'re not organizing** the sales conference this year.
Is Uschi **running** the training course? Yes, she **is**.

Use To talk about temporary activities or activities happening 'around now'.
N.B. Verbs which express a state (e.g. **know**, **like**, **want**) are usually used with the present simple, even if we are talking about 'now'.

Past simple tense

She **leased** a building in Sydney.
She **didn't start** her business in Melbourne.
Did she **go** to Japan last year? Yes, she **did**.

Irregular verbs

begin	began	begun	give	gave	given	see	saw	seen
buy	bought	bought	go	went	gone	sell	sold	sold
come	came	come	leave	left	left	speak	spoke	spoken
do	did	done	make	made	made	take	took	taken
find	found	found	meet	met	met	tell	told	told
fly	flew	flown	put	put	put	think	thought	thought
get	got	got	say	said	said	write	wrote	written

Use To talk about completed actions in the past.
N.B. We often use time markers (e.g. yesterday, two years ago) with the past simple.

Useful words and expressions

Introductions
How do you do?
Pleased to meet you.
Do you know *Ms Lee*?
Have you met *Mr Tan*?

Greetings
How are you?
Fine, thanks.
Not too bad.

What do you do?
Who do you work for?

I agree.
I don't agree.
headquarters
main markets
employees
manufacture
market
I'm responsible for *quality control*.
He's in charge of *Sales*.
They deal with *customer complaints*.

Correspondence
Thank you for your letter of *3 June*.
We enclose *a catalogue and price list*.
Please contact me *for further details*.

On the phone
I'd like to speak to *Mr Bird*.
Could you put me through to *Ms Greene*?
There's no reply.
The line's engaged.
Would you like to leave a message?
Can I take a message?
Who's calling?

Inviting people to do things
Would you like to …?
How about … ing?
I'd love to.
That sounds great.

Talking about your interests
I'm interested in …
I'm not really interested in …
I quite like …
I don't really like …

You might also find it helpful to make lists of the following vocabulary:
industries, departments and jobs which are important for your work, and your
free time activities.

AIMS

Talk about infrastructure
Describe facilities
Compare advantages and disadvantages
Deal with orders

Comparative and superlative adjectives

Adjectives describing quality

Punctuation and capitalization

6 Transportation

6.1 Describing infrastructure

A Look at the picture and find the following:

airport   truck[1]   railroad[2]   highway[3]   port   cargo ship   tanker   container
freight train[4]

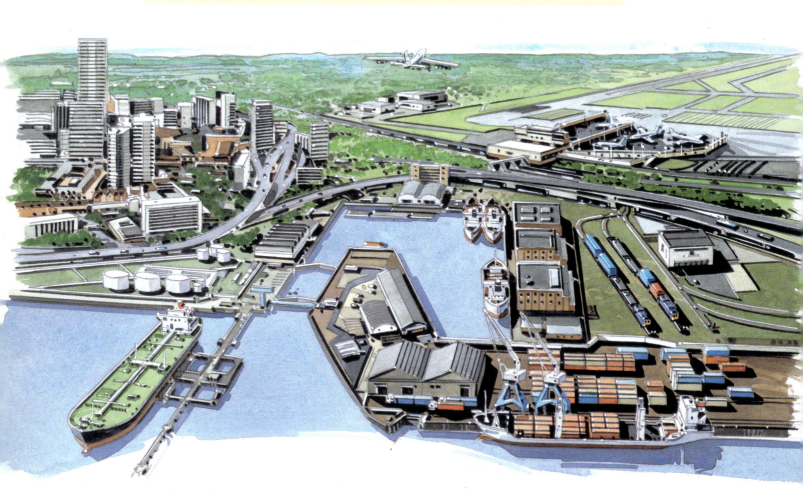

British English: [1]lorry; [2]railway; [3]motorway; [4]goods train

B Read this article about Virginia. How many different forms of transport are mentioned?

Virginia, USA

Virginia is fast becoming the transportation hub of the eastern USA. .... (1)

And our 14 commercial airports put us within easy reach of practically every major city in the world. We offer supersonic transport service with Concorde to London and Paris. Non-stop flights to Frankfurt and Tokyo. Direct flights to Moscow, Jeddah, Stuttgart, Warsaw and Geneva. .... (2)

Our seaports are equally top flight. More goods are exported through the Port at Hampton Roads than any other seaport in the country. The cargo handling facilities at Hampton Roads Port are the most advanced in the world. .... (3)

We also have important railroad links. .... (4)

We have the third largest highway system in the United States, almost 54,000 miles. .... (5)

When it comes to transportation, no other state delivers like Virginia.

These sentences are missing from the article. Where do you think they belong?

a We also offer non-stop flights to 65 domestic destinations.
b There are also plans to add $10 billion worth of new roads and highway improvements.
c Our location in the center of the eastern seaboard puts us within 500 miles of half the population of the United States.
d More than 80 shipping lines link the harbor with 270 ports in 100 different countries.
e Virginia is the junction point for major north–south and east–west lines.

C These words can be used to say how good the facilities are. Put them under the correct heading like this:

adequate   terrible   first class   fair   poor   excellent   satisfactory   very good
unsatisfactory

+++	+/–	– – –
....	*adequate*	....
....	....	....
....	....	....

What are the transport links like for industry where you live? Describe them using the words above.

D Find out about the transport facilities in Sydney, Australia and Singapore. Learner A looks at File 13 on page 118 and Learner B looks at File 14 on page 122.

6.2 Forms of transport

A 📼 ◎ Listen to someone from Transworld Freight Forwarders talking about different types of transport and complete the grid.

Transport	Advantage	Disadvantage
a	fast	expensive large quantities not possible
b	suitable for heavy goods or large quantities	.... ports expensive delays common
c	door-to-door service	....
d	economical use of labour	no door-to-door service

B Study these ways of comparing things.

> Transporting goods by air is much fast**er than** by sea.
> Transporting goods by sea is **not as** fast **as** by air.
> Transporting goods by air is **the** fast**est** method.

> Transporting goods by air is **more** expensive **than** by sea.
> Transporting goods by sea is **not as** expensive **as** by air.
> Transporting goods by air is **the most** expensive method.

N.B. good − better − best; bad − worse − worst

Make some sentences comparing air and road transport. Use the words in the box to help you like this:

Transporting goods by air isn't as cheap as by road.

> cheap   fast   difficult   dangerous   slow   expensive   easy   safe

Which method of transport is

a the most flexible?
b the most reliable?
c the most environmentally friendly?

Compare your answers with a partner.

C Match the type of cargo to the symbol.

Types of cargo	
1 perishable goods	☐
2 hazardous goods	☐
3 livestock	☐
4 high value cargo	☐
5 fragile goods	☐
6 flammable goods	☐

a   b   c

d   e   f

Can you think of other examples of these types of cargo?

D **You work for a consultancy firm. Write short reports on the best methods of transport for your clients.**

1 Leuwan Florist of Holland deals in flowers and supplies the European market.
2 Johnson Chemicals of Britain distributes chemicals to the European market.
3 Heriot Meats of New Zealand supplies the Middle East and Japan with livestock and frozen meat.
4 ACR of Taiwan supplies the world market with computer monitors.

Don't forget to give reasons for and against the different means of transport.

6.3 Dealing with an order

A You are Brian Davison's assistant at VAC Industries. Look at this fax and fill in the missing information in the header.

28 August   Spain   Ms Sanchez   Royale Engineering Company

VAC Industries

28 Devon Road,
Plymouth
PL1 1HZ

Fax: ++44 (0)1752 323821
Tel: ++44 (0)1752 328822

Attention : ....
Company : ....
Country : ....
From   : Brian Davison
Date   : ....

dear ms sanchez

thank you for your order of 23 august we are pleased to confirm your order of 20 units of model 1203 payment by letter of credit we will deliver the goods by 20 september by ship to bilbao i will send you shipping details on Monday

i look forward to hearing from you soon

yours sincerely

brian davison
marketing manager

Look at the rest of the fax and add capitals and full stops.

B Listen to Ms Sanchez calling VAC Industries. What does she want to change?

payment conditions   ☐
number of machines ordered ☐
method of delivery   ☐
model of machine   ☐

C This is the memo Brian Davison sent to the dispatch department. Is it correct?

MEMO

Change delivery conditions (Royale Engineering Ms Sanchez)
– order no. E 5490.

   Air freight to Bilbao as soon as possible.
   Ms Sanchez to pay additional freight costs.

D Brian Davison has asked you to write to Ms Sanchez confirming the changes. Look at these sentences. Which two can you use?

1 Please send me the information as soon as possible.
2 Additional charges for delivery by air freight will be paid by you.
3 Thank you for your enquiry.
4 Please find enclosed information on terms of payment and conditions of delivery.
5 We have arranged for the immediate dispatch of the goods by air freight.

Now write a fax confirming the new arrangements.

VAC Industries

28 Devon Road,
Plymouth
PL1 1HZ

Fax: ++44 (0)1752 323821
Tel: ++44 (0)1752 328822

Attention : ....
Company : ....
Country   : ....
From   : ....
Date   : ....

Message

AIMS

Talk about imports and exports
Talk about quantity
Describe change: past and present

Quantity
Mass and count nouns

Past time
Past simple and present perfect

7 Imports and exports

7.1 Talking about industries

A Match these industries to the icons below and write them in the blanks.

textile   automobile   pharmaceutical   computer   chemical   tourism   petroleum
agriculture

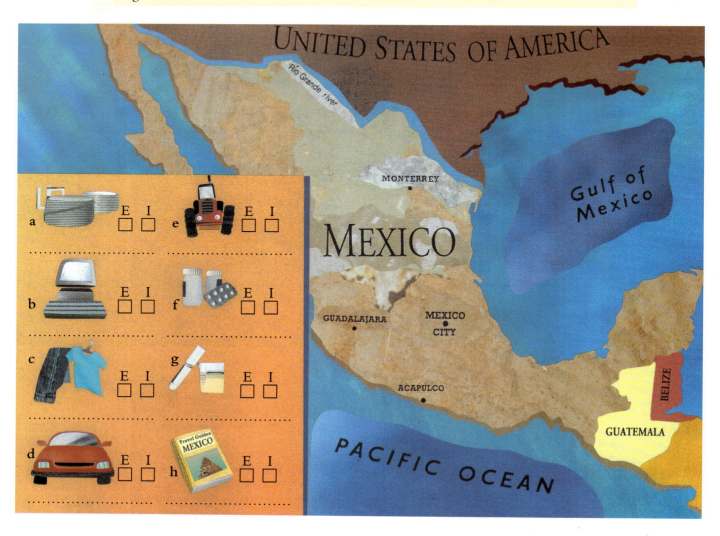

B 📼 ◎ **Listen to an interview with a Mexican businessman.**
Are the industries in **A** exports (E) or imports (I)? Tick the boxes as you listen.

Listen again. What industry does he work in?

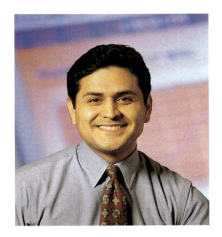

C Look at these types of industries. Can you explain each type?

Commodities	Manufacturing	Services
oil	textiles	tourism and travel

Put these industries into the correct column.

> consumer electronics   advertising   oil   rice   pharmaceuticals   coffee   retailing
> banking   coal   furniture   textiles   cars   insurance   wool   tourism and travel

D Make a list of important industries in your area or country. Then compare with a partner.

You can use these expressions to help you:

> *The main industry is …*
> *Our major export is …*
> *We are developing the … industry/business.*
> *Other important service/manufacturing industries are …*
> *… employs a lot of people in my area.*

7.2 Talking about imports and exports

A This chart shows South Korean imports from China.

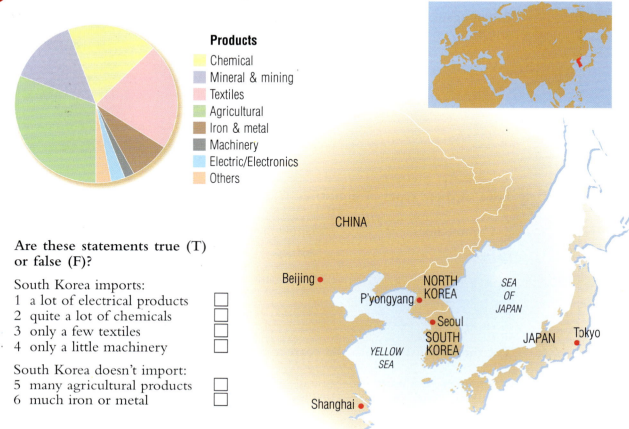

Products
- Chemical
- Mineral & mining
- Textiles
- Agricultural
- Iron & metal
- Machinery
- Electric/Electronics
- Others

Are these statements true (T) or false (F)?

South Korea imports:
1 a lot of electrical products ☐
2 quite a lot of chemicals ☐
3 only a few textiles ☐
4 only a little machinery ☐

South Korea doesn't import:
5 many agricultural products ☐
6 much iron or metal ☐

B Study these ways of talking about quantity.

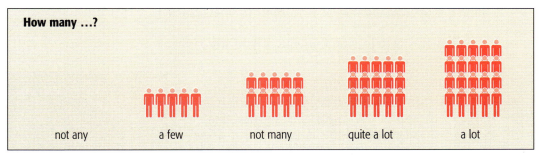

Now complete these conversations, using words from above.

A: How .....*much*.....(1) does your country earn from tourism each year?
B: I don't know exactly, but I'd say ....(2).

A: How ....(3) tourists visit your country each year?
B: I can't really say, but I think ....(4).

A: Do you import ....(5) coal?
B: No, ...(6).

A: Do you export ....(7) cars?
B: No, only ....(8).

C This pie chart shows
South Korean exports to China.
Make some sentences like this:

South Korea exports a lot of ....

- Textiles
- Iron & metal
- Machinery
- Electric/Electronics
- Chemical
- Mineral & mining
- Others

D Practise finding out about a country's imports and exports. Learner A looks at
File 15 on page 121 and Learner B looks at File 16 on page 124.

A Look at these statements about American manufacturing in the 1980s. Do you think they are true (T) or false (F)?

In the 1980s, American companies:
1 had an international outlook. ☐
2 still used old-fashioned methods of production. ☐
3 took a short-term view of business. ☐
4 were good at developing new products. ☐
5 neglected human resources. ☐
6 didn't cooperate effectively with their business partners. ☐

Now read this article and find out if you are right.

THEN

1 **Then** American firms relied too much on the domestic market, despite increasing competition from Europe and Japan. They were blind to science and innovation outside the USA and therefore failed to adapt foreign discoveries for use at home. ☐

2 **Then** American industry continued to mass produce goods long after the Japanese had learnt that not only economies of scale but also quality, reliability and different products for different segments of the market are important. ☐

3 **Then** American firms had short-time horizons. While Japanese companies invested heavily in consumer technologies, American consumer electronics firms diversified into other businesses such as car rentals and financial services. They eventually lost the market altogether. ☐

4 **Then** there was too much emphasis on 'basic research' and too little on the technical work needed to turn brilliant ideas into products that people would buy. Designers didn't bother to make sure products could be manufactured easily and reliably. The art of manufacturing was not respected. ☐

5 **Then** on-the-job training in Germany and Japan gave these countries an advantage over American firms. These did not try to improve workers' skills. ☐

6 **Then** American firms were bad at cooperating. Both customer–supplier relations and labour relations were poor. ☐

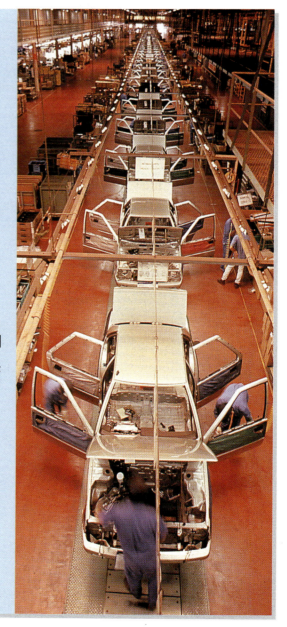

B Now match a paragraph from this article on American manufacturing in the 1990s to a paragraph from **A**.

NOW

a **Now** firms as well as universities have begun to take manufacturing more seriously. More engineers, and better ones, work in manufacturing. 'We realized you couldn't just invent', says a senior vice-president at Intel. 'You also had to make a few million things.'

b **Now** no big firm ignores its suppliers any more.

c **Now** American manufacturers, in the middle of an export boom, are focused on the outside world. The number of exporting businesses has increased. Many firms are looking for openings in Russia, China, India or Brazil.

d **Now** the biggest American companies say that people are their most valuable resource. Since 1982, 80,000 Ford workers have been through training programmes. Chaparral Steel tries to keep 85% of its employees enrolled in training courses at any time.

e **Now** from Coca-Cola to Fidelity Investments, American companies have learnt to segment the market. They have also discovered continuous quality improvement. In 1994, AT&T became the first American company to win Japan's Deming prize for quality control. Many companies have introduced quality raising initiatives.

f **Now** American firms have begun to take a longer view. Shareholders are behaving more like long-term owners and managers are more accountable for their performance.

© The Economist

C Study these ways of talking about the past.

Past simple (then)	Present perfect (result now)
American firms **relied** on the domestic market. American firms **did not try** to improve workers' skills.	The number of exporting firms **has increased**. 80,000 Ford workers **have been** on training programmes.

Read this article about an American rail company and <u>underline</u> the correct tense.

AT YOUR SERVICE

Southern Pacific is now the sixth-biggest rail company by revenue. In 1980, it *employed / has employed* (1) 30,000 people. Now it has 18,000. Under the ownership of a Denver billionaire, the company *invested / has invested* (2) heavily in new technology. It *consolidated / has consolidated* (3) many of its operations and *sold / has sold* (4) some of its track. A further 4,000 employees *lost / have lost* (5) their jobs last year, but revenue ton-miles per employee *went up / has gone up* (6) last year to 7.5m from 4.3m in 1990.

D Work in small groups. Make notes on your area or company ten years ago. What has changed since then? Compare your ideas with another group.

AIMS

Talk about schedules
Make and change arrangements and appointments
Deal with correspondence
Make a telephone call to arrange a meeting

Future time
Present progressive for future
will future

8 Arrangements

8.1 Discussing an itinerary

A What arrangements have to be made before someone goes on a business trip abroad? Make a list.

B 📼 ◎ Olivia Miller is going to Bombay on business. Listen to her discussing the trip with her secretary and complete the itinerary.

Olivia Miller – Trip to Bombay

Monday, October 3rd

.... Car to London Heathrow, Terminal 4
.... BA Flight 139 to Bombay
.... Arrive Bombay, transfer to hotel

Tuesday, October 4th

.... Meeting with Mr Shah

Wednesday, October 5th

All day   Tour of new plant in Bombay and meeting with directors

Thursday, October 6th

.... BA flight 138 to London Heathrow
.... Arrive London Heathrow
.... Sales meeting, London

C Study these ways of talking about the future.

Present progressive (for arrangements)
I'm **arriving** on Monday.
You're **seeing** him at 2.00.
She's **staying** at the Oberoi.

Will (for sudden decisions and promises)	
	make an appointment.
I'll	ask my boss.
	confirm it at once.

Complete this conversation with the correct form of the verb. Use the verbs in the box to help you.

come   fly   see   fax   stay

OLIVIA: When ....(1) to New York?

ASSISTANT: Friday morning. Your flight's at nine o'clock.

OLIVIA: Where ....(2)?

ASSISTANT: At the Royalton Hotel. I'm afraid the Plaza is full.

OLIVIA: When ....(3) Bill Urwin?

ASSISTANT: Friday afternoon at four o'clock, local time.

OLIVIA: ....

                 Neil ....(4) to the meeting too?

ASSISTANT: Yes, he is.

OLIVIA: Good, but he needs a copy of the report for it.

ASSISTANT: Right. ....(5) it this afternoon.

D Practise talking about schedules. Learner A looks at File 17 on page 118 and Learner B looks at File 18 on page 122.

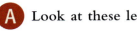 **A** Look at these letters. Which one is:

a thanking   b arranging   c confirming   d inviting   e accepting   f cancelling

1 ☐

February 2, 199-

Dear Mr Oliver Schmutz:

I am pleased to be able to invite you to the Annual Conference of Packagers, which will take place in Los Angeles 4 – 7 July.

I enclose a program with details of the speakers and the various topics that have been proposed, together with a registration form. On receipt of your form we will send you details of accommodation in Los Angeles, together with a booking form. Any further enquiries should be sent to me at the above address.

I look forward to seeing you in Los Angeles in July.

Sincerely,

Sheila Legl

2 ☐

February 5, 199-

Dear Oliver

Thank you very much for your hospitality while I was in Portland.
   It was very useful to see the new warehouse and I hope to be able to implement some of your suggestions here in Germany.
   I look forward to seeing you when you come to Frankfurt in the fall.

Best regards

Dieter

3 ☐

February 9, 199-

Dear Mr Schmutz:

Unfortunately Ms Gilbertson is not able to keep the appointment with you on Wednesday, February 11 at 2.20 as an urgent matter will prevent her from travelling to Portland.

Please accept her apologies. She will contact you as soon as she returns to HQ.

4 ☐

February 11, 199-

Dear Mr Schmutz:

We are pleased to confirm your reservation for one single room with bath from February 22 to 24.

Please let us know your time of arrival and departure.

Sincerely yours,

5 ☐

February 9, 199-

Dear Sir/Madam:

Please reserve a single room with bath for the nights of February 22, 23, 24.

I would be grateful if you could confirm my reservation.

Sincerely,

Oliver Schmutz

6 ☐

February 8, 199-

Dear Mr Riddlestone:

Thank you for your invitation to attend the opening of your new training center.

I would be most pleased to attend and look forward to seeing you there.

Best regards,

Oliver Schmutz

Reread the letters and <u>underline</u> the words and expressions that helped you get the answers.

B These expressions are often used in correspondence.

Requesting

Could you please *confirm my reservation*?
We would be grateful if you could *return the booking form today*.

Giving good news

I am pleased to *invite you to the annual conference*.

Giving bad news

Unfortunately, *Ms Gilbertson is not able to meet you*.
I am afraid *we will not be able to meet as planned*.

Thanking

Thank you for *your hospitality*.
We were pleased to *see you last week*.

Confirming

I confirm *your meeting next Thursday*.
I am pleased to confirm *your reservation for next week*.

Now rewrite these phrases to make them more polite like this:

I would be grateful if you could cancel my reservation.

1 Cancel my reservation.
2 Mr Petersen can come to the reception on 1 May.
3 Mrs Lindgren can't come to the reception on 1 May.
4 I want an appointment on 22 May.
5 Send me confirmation of my booking.
6 Thanks for dinner last week.

C 📼 ◎ **Listen to Jeff Morgan discussing a business trip to Orlando.**

1 When is he travelling to Orlando?
   a 9 January   b 19 January   c 29 January
2 How many nights does he want to stay there?
   a 1 night   b 2 nights   c 3 nights
3 When is the meeting with Orion?
   a 1 February   b 5 February   c 21 January

D You are Jeff Morgan's assistant. Write a fax to the Marriot Hotel and a fax to Orion for him.

8.3 Making and changing an appointment

A ▭ ◎ This is Kate Williams' diary. Listen to two phone calls and fill in the appointments.

October

	MON. **10**
	TUE. **11**
Present new brochures	WED. **12**
2.30 Mr. Bloch	THUR. **13**
9.0 Printer's	FRI. **14**
	SAT. **15**
	SUN. **16**

B Study these ways of making an appointment.

Suggesting a time

When would | be convenient?
| suit you?

Are you free on *Monday*?
How about *10.00*?

Saying *yes*

That's fine.
That suits me.

Saying *no*

I'm afraid I can't make | *Wednesday.*
I'm sorry, I can't manage | *the morning.*

Now practise this conversation with a partner.

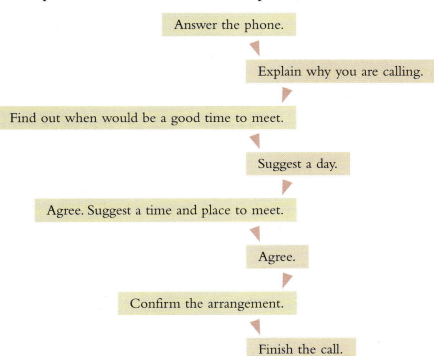

Answer the phone.

Explain why you are calling.

Find out when would be a good time to meet.

Suggest a day.

Agree. Suggest a time and place to meet.

Agree.

Confirm the arrangement.

Finish the call.

C Kate Williams phones Ian Norman to change their appointment. What do you think she will say to him?

Now listen and write the new appointment in her diary.

D Practise making and changing arrangements. Learner A looks at File 19 on page 117, Learner B looks at File 20 on page 120.

AIMS

Describe a product
Make and deal with complaints
Apologize

Adjectives
materials/shapes/qualities

9 Products and services

9.1 Services

 A Read this leaflet about First Direct. What services does it offer?

Welcome to a new and different way of banking

First Direct offers a banking service that enables you to do all your normal banking business without having to set foot inside a bank branch.

First Direct is a division of Midland Bank plc and offers a person to person banking service 24 hours a day, every day – at the end of a telephone. Your call will always be answered by a banking representative whose job is to assist you with a full range of banking products and services. Our interest rates are highly competitive because our overheads are low. We have no branches so we can pass on cost savings to our customers.

The banking service that gives you time for the important things in life

First Direct lets you make more of your time. Whether you are busy at work, or relaxing at home, the UK's first 24-hour person-to-person banking service is more convenient.

It lets you manage your finances whenever you want. You can call us at any time of the day or night, at weekends, even on public holidays, for a wide range of banking services.

You can call us 24 hours a day to arrange payment of domestic bills (gas, electricity, water, etc.); transfer money in the UK or around the world; check the balance of your Cheque Account, or order foreign currency or travellers' cheques.

Make the most of your time with a First Direct Cheque Account.

Why you should bank with First Direct

- We are open 24 hours a day, every day.
- You can transact your banking needs over the telephone.
- You can pay bills over the telephone.
- You can withdraw up to £500 cash a day from over 13,500 cash machines.
- You can guarantee cheques up to £100.
- You will always deal with friendly and efficient staff.

Read the leaflet again and correct these statements.

a First Direct has branches in all major cities.
b The bank is open from 8 a.m. to 8 p.m.
c Bank charges are higher than in other banks.
d It offers only a limited range of services.
e You can withdraw £500 a week from cash machines in the UK.
f You can guarantee cheques up to £50.

What do you think? Would you like to use First Direct as a bank? Does your bank offer a similar service?

B Match a word or phrase in the leaflet with these definitions:

a to enter a building
b the local office of an organization
c a company which is part of a large group
d the person from the bank you will speak to
e money you get when you deposit money with the bank
f money spent on the day-to-day costs of a business.

C Listen to a phone call between First Direct and a potential customer. What does he want to know?

D You are going to role play some phone calls to First Direct. Learner A looks at File 23 on page 119 and Learner B looks at File 24 on page 124.

When you have practised your role plays, act them out for another pair. Ask them if they think you are friendly, helpful and efficient!

A Look at this bed. What questions can you ask to complete the missing information?

Length: ....
Width: ....
Height: ....
Colours: ....
Material: ....
Price: ....

B Listen to a sales representative describing the bed to a potential customer and complete the missing information. What are the advantages of this range of furniture?

C Look at these words for describing a product.

robust plastic easy-to-use metal round wood attractive leather square
sphere cotton wool cube good-value cone triangle flexible long-lasting

Put them into categories like this:

Shape	Material	Quality
round	plastic	robust

Use some of the words above to describe something in your bag or pockets.

D Practise describing some products. Learner A looks at File 27 on page 116 and Learner B looks at File 28 on page 120.

9.3 Keeping the customer happy

A 🔲 ◎ You work in the Sales Department at Leroy Motors. Listen to a colleague phoning the printers. What is the problem?

Now listen to the printer returning your colleague's call. Which brochures is she waiting for? When will she get them?

B The brochures have now arrived. Read this letter your colleague has written to a customer. Why has she written it?

LEROY
MOTORS INC

**199 Heidelberg Rd,
Ivanhoe,
Victoria 3177**

Ho Industries
Attn: Mr Peter Wong
Shoei Yuan Road
Taipei
Taiwan, ROC

April 27, 199-

Dear Mr Wong

I apologize for the delay in sending you information on our complete range of industrial motors. This was because some of the brochures were still at the printers.

Please find enclosed the missing brochures on our models in the A90 range.

I hope this did not cause any inconvenience. Please accept my apologies again.

Best regards

Jennifer Austin

Jennifer Austin
Sales Manager

Read the letter again. <u>Underline</u> the phrases the writer uses to apologize.

C Study these ways of apologizing and accepting an apology.

Apologizing

I'm | very / really | sorry.

Accepting an apology

I see.
That's OK.
Never mind.

Practise making apologies. Role play this phone call between another customer who is still waiting for the brochures and yourself.

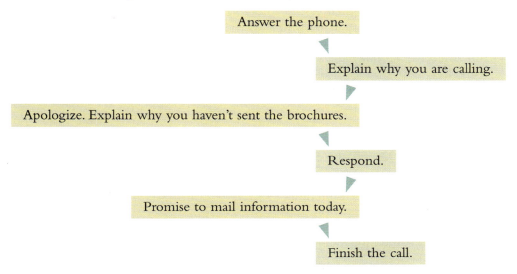

Answer the phone.

Explain why you are calling.

Apologize. Explain why you haven't sent the brochures.

Respond.

Promise to mail information today.

Finish the call.

D ▭ ◎ Listen to some voice-mails. What are the problems? First decide if you will write or call the customer. Then role play the call or draft the letter.

Message	Problem	Action
1	....	....
2	....	....
3	....	....

10 Revision and consolidation

A Grammar Correct the mistakes in these sentences.

a Is it more quick to transport goods by rail or by road?
b Which is the expensivist method of transport?
c We import much computers but we don't import much machinery.
d How much cars do you export each year?
e Unemployment has increased during the eighties.
f Transport improved a lot. We now have a new rail link.
g When go you to headquarters?
h How much nights do you want to stay?
i I booking a room for you at the Sheraton.
j I'm afraid Mr Honda can't come to the meeting because he will go on a course on Thursday.
k How much weigh those shelves over there?
l It's 3.5 metres length.

B What do you say? Match the function to the actual words.

1 Describe facilities.
2 Ask about the price of something.
3 Talk about arrangements.
4 Offer help.
5 Offer to do something.
6 Apologize.
7 Describe a product.
8 Suggest a time for a meeting.

a I'll meet you at the station.
b What can I do for you?
c Would Thursday morning suit you?
d What does it cost?
e It's excellent value-for-money.
f The airport is excellent.
g I'm sorry. What exactly is the problem?
h I'm seeing Mr Honda on Tuesday.

Now write a short dialogue using some of these phrases.

C Vocabulary Put these words into three categories and then give them a heading.

tanker oil insurance truck port plastic container leather chemicals
wood tourism cotton

Add some more words to each category.

D 🔲 ◎ **Listening** This chart shows why people change banks.

Now listen to James Shaw explaining why he changed banks. Which reasons does he mention? What other reasons not in the chart does he give?

The Sunday Times 25 February 1996

E **Reading** Read this article about changing banks and put these steps in the right order:

- [ ] Cut your cheque-guarantee card in half.
- [ ] Tell the new bank to take over payment of the standing orders and direct debits.
- [ ] Write a letter to the old bank to close the account.
- [ ] Instruct your employer to pay your salary into the new account.
- [ ] Ask your old bank to send you a list of standing-order and direct-debit commitments.
- [ ] Cancel the payment of standing orders with the old bank.

THE ITCH TO SWITCH

by Naomi Caine

Dissatisfied with your bank? Many people are, but few actually move.

According to a recent survey, about 36 million of us run a current account, but more than 6 million of us are dissatisfied with our bank.

Excessive charges and poor service are the most common complaints. But we also grumble about low interest rates for accounts in credit, too few cash points and inconvenient branch opening hours and location.

If you get the itch to switch, the first step is to instruct your employer to pay your salary into the new account – give at least one month's notice.

Next, ask your bank to send you a list of direct-debit and standing-order commitments. Tell your new bank to take over the payment of the standing orders and then cancel them with the old bank.

Dealing with direct debits is more difficult. You must send a letter to everyone you pay by direct debit to let them know you are changing banks. They will then send new direct-debit forms, which you must complete and return before you cancel the old direct-debits.

Once all payments into and out of your old account have been switched to your new one, cut your old cheque-guarantee card in half and send it to your old bank, together with any unused cheques and a letter to close the account.

The whole process can take up to two months – and things can go wrong. Direct debts may be paid twice, or missed altogether. Customers may also find that payments go out of the account before the salary has gone in. Unless the bank offers free overdraft facilities you could pay the price for being in the red.

The Sunday Times 25 February 1996

Summary

Comparison

	Adjective	Comparative			Superlative
One syllable	cheap	cheap**er**			cheap**est**
One syllable + y	easy	eas**ier**	**than**	**the**	eas**iest**
Two or more syllables	reliable	**more** reliable			**most** reliable

Comparative

We are **cheaper than** our competitors. We are also **more reliable**.
Transworld are **the fastest** freight forwarders. They are also **the most expensive**.
We are **as flexible as** our competitors.

Quantity

	Uncountable nouns	Countable nouns
+++	a little, some, a lot of	a few, some, a lot of
– – –	not much, any	not many, any
???	How much?	How many?

We export **a little** rice and we import **a few** trucks.
We do **not** export **any** oil and we do **not** import **any** cars.
How much wheat do you export? **How many** buses do you import?

Present perfect tense

Present perfect	Past simple
We**'ve made** 100,000 widgets.	We **made** 10,000 widgets **in April**.
We **haven't sold** all of them yet.	We **didn't sell** any **last month**.
Have you **confirmed** that order?	When **did** you **confirm** it?

Use   We use the present perfect to talk about past actions when we are thinking about the result now.

N.B. If we are talking about a definite time in the past (e.g. yesterday, last week, two years ago) we use the past simple and **not** the present perfect.

The future

Present progressive	Will
I**'m flying** to New York on Monday.	Have you confirmed my flight yet? No, I haven't. I**'ll do** it now.
We**'re not staying** at the Hilton.	I still have a lot of travellers' cheques. OK, I **won't order** any more.
Is your boss **coming** to the meeting?	

Use   We use the present progressive to talk about future arrangements.
We use *will* for decisions and promises made at the time of speaking.

Useful words and expressions

Your translation

airport ....
cargo ship ....
container ....
courier ....
goods train/freight train★ ....
lorry/truck★ ....
railway/railroad★ ....
motorway/highway★ ....
port ....
tanker ....

adequate ....
excellent ....
fair ....
poor ....
unsatisfactory ....
terrible ....

flexible ....
reliable ....
environmentally friendly ....

arrange a meeting ....
confirm a booking ....
accept an invitation ....
cancel an appointment ....

height ....
length ....
width ....
weight ....

Making appointments
When would be convenient? ....
When would suit you? ....
Are you free on *Monday*? ....
How about *10.00*? ....
That's fine. ....
That suits me. ....
I'm afraid I can't make *Wednesday*. ....
I'm sorry, I can't manage *the morning*. ....

Correspondence
Please could you *send us a price list*. ....
I am pleased to *invite you* … ....
I am afraid that *I will not be able to attend* … ....
I apologize for *the delay*. ....
Unfortunately *there was a problem* … ....
Please accept my apologies. ....

You might also find it helpful to make lists of the following vocabulary: industries which are important for your country, types of cargo, shapes, adjectives to describe your company's products, and materials.

★American English

11 **Marketing**

11.1 Projecting an image

A Look at these two logos for the British Broadcasting Corporation (BBC). Which one do you prefer? Why?

These logos are trade marks of the British Broadcasting Corporation and are used under licence.

B ⬛ ◎ Now listen to someone from the BBC talking about the two logos and answer these questions.

1 Why did the BBC decide to change its logo?
2 What were the problems with the old logo?
3 What were the aims of the new logo?
4 What has it cost the BBC to change the logo?

C Look at this company's printed and marketing material. What are the different branded items?

Which of these items are used as promotional materials?

D Study these ways of defining objects.

who/that = people (not things)	**which/that = things**
A customer is someone **who** buys something from a company.	An invoice is something **which** asks for payment of goods or services.

Choose an ending to make sentences about the items on the left like this:

A catalogue is something which lists items for sale and their prices.

1	catalogue	prints books and leaflets
2	newsletter	is printed at the top of writing paper
3	supplier	is used on products and advertising material
4	letterhead	gives news about a company
5	graphic designer	lists items for sale and their prices
6	logo	designs logos, etc.
7	printer	provides a company with goods or equipment

A There are many different ways of promoting a product. How and where are these two products advertised?

B Read this extract from an article on different ways of promoting goods and services. Put in the correct terms.

Direct mail   Advertising   Merchandising   Consumer promotions

Special offers, discounts and free offer and sample coupons are all examples of .... (1) They can persuade consumers to try a product for the first time, to change from a competitive product or to increase the size of a purchase.

.... (2) consists of giving away or selling useful objects, such as sports bags or shopping holdalls with your brand name. You can also associate a character, personality or animal with your products and produce stickers, key rings, pens or other giveaway items to help people connect this image with your business.

.... (3) is promotional communicating by post. It is whatever the sender wants it to be – advertising, market research or a 'thank you' letter to customers.

It is useful where a product or service has a limited customer base because it addresses named targets only. It can be extremely cost-effective. It is also flexible in size, content and timing. It is most effective when it is linked with other opportunities to communicate. You can follow it up by telephone, meeting or other forms of advertising.

Although .... (4) is very expensive, it is an economical way of getting a message to a large audience. If considering a magazine, study its circulation carefully. How many people does it go to? Are they people who might buy from you? What other advertisers does the magazine have? Local radio and regional television can be affordable. However, remember they are best suited to consumer goods and not industrial or business products, where needs must be more closely targeted.

C Now reread the article. Are these statements true (T) or false (F)?

1 One of the aims of sales promotions is to get customers to buy new products. ☐
2 Special offers, discounts and free samples are all forms of merchandising. ☐
3 If you have only a small number of customers, direct mail is ideal. ☐
4 Direct mail is a very expensive way of promoting a product or service. ☐
5 Radio and TV are cost-effective means of advertising. ☐
6 Radio and TV are ideal for advertising industrial products. ☐

D Work in groups. You work for an international advertising agency and have to prepare an advertising campaign for these products in your country. First, think about the potential customers and where the product is sold. Where would you advertise them? Why would you choose these media over others? Write a short report giving your suggestions, then compare with other learners.

A 🔲 ◎ You work in the Marketing Department of Niche Wear, a clothing store for young adults and children. You have a reputation for good quality at a reasonable price and are expanding rapidly.

In six weeks you are opening another store. Listen to this message your boss has left you and make notes.

PROMOTIONAL CAMPAIGN FOR NEW STORE

Promotional gifts for:

No. of items:

Budget:

Other:

B Look at this catalogue and choose products for the promotional campaign.

BALLPOINT PENS

Blue, yellow, green, red, black, white

200 23p each
500 21p each
1000 19p each

KEYRINGS

Blue, red, yellow, white, black or green

200 57p each
500 54p each
1000 52p each

ERASERS

Blue, black, white, red or yellow

250 25p each
500 22p each
1000 19p each

BALLOONS

Assorted colours and shapes

1000 12p each
5000 7p each
10000 5p each

REFLECTORS

Bear or cat motifs in blue, green, orange

100 49p each
250 45p each
1000 37p each

BASEBALL CAPS

100% cotton
Adjustable strap
Colour: white

100 £1.79 each
250 £1.74 each
500 £1.69 each

PENKNIVES

Blue, yellow, green, red, black, white

150 £1.39 each
250 £1.34 each
500 £1.24 each

SPACE FLYERS

220mm. White, blue, red, green, yellow

500 64p each
1000 59p each
2500 54p each

C   Now complete this order form for the products you have chosen.

Quantity ....   Product ....   Product colour ....

Quantity ....   Product ....   Product colour ....

Quantity ....   Product ....   Product colour ....

Quantity ....   Product ....   Product colour ....

Quantity ....   Product ....   Product colour ....

Print colour ....

Company name ....   Name of buyer ....

Address ....

....

Postcode ....   Tel. ....   Fax ....

D   These sentences can be used in the letter to accompany your order form. First match the beginnings and endings. Then draft a letter to accompany your order form.

Please confirm ...   ... receiving the goods.

We would like to ...   ... you can deliver the goods within ... days.

We enclose ...   ... place an order for the following items.

We look forward to ...   ... your official order form.

12 **Statistics**

AIMS

Describe trends
Talk about cause and effect
Give reasons for changes in performance
Discuss training programmes
Make a short presentation

Adjectives and adverbs

Sequencing language

12.1 Describing performance

A Read these extracts from Volvo's annual report and match each one to a graph.

1 Sales of cars were 2 per cent lower than last year. In Europe, sales increased by less than 2 per cent to 197,000 cars. Market shares were just under 2 per cent. In North America, the number of cars sold remained unchanged. In other markets, sales declined slightly. The number of cars sold in Japan fell 15 per cent to 8,600 units. Sales in Southeast Asia increased to 10,700 units.

2 Sales of trucks were down 9 per cent compared with last year's figures. Volvo delivered a total of 48,130 trucks of which 5,100 were medium-heavy units and 43,000 were in the heavy class. In Europe, the number of heavy trucks sold decreased by 21 per cent to 18,400 and the share of the total market in Europe shrank slightly to 12 per cent. In North America, sales followed the upturn in the market and deliveries rose 25 per cent to 16,720. In other markets, sales of trucks dropped by 4,020 to 8,180 units.

3 Sales of buses increased by 16 per cent over the preceding year. Deliveries of buses rose 20 per cent to a total of 5,580 vehicles. In Europe, Volvo delivered a total of 2,360 buses. The market share fell slightly from 14 to 12 per cent. Volvo buses are not marketed in North America. In other markets, the number of buses sold climbed to 3,230, a dramatic increase of 45 per cent.

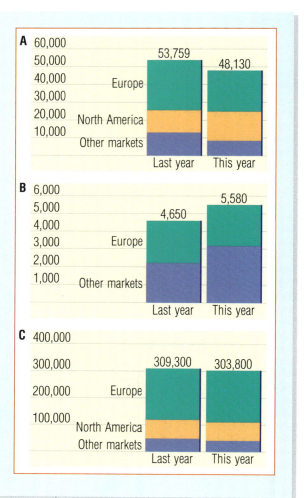

Reread the texts. <u>Underline</u> all the words and phrases which describe an upward (↑) or downward (↓) movement.

B These verbs describe trends. Put them under the correct heading like this:

> to soar   to drop   to remain unchanged   to decline   to rise   to decrease   to jump
> to remain stable   to climb   to plunge   to fall   to increase

↑↑	↑	↑/↓	↓	↓↓
to soar				

These words describe the degree of change. Group them like this:

> gradually   suddenly   slowly   steadily   slightly   dramatically   sharply

+	++	+++
gradually		

This table shows sales of trucks around the world. Write some sentences like this:

Sales in Brazil fell slightly.

	Last year	This year
Brazil	1,070	950
Iran	470	470
Uruguay	50	470
Singapore	0	300
Sweden	360	290
Peru	150	220

C Study the difference between adjectives and adverbs.

Adjectives				Adverbs		
There was a	sharp	increase	in sales.	Sales	increased	sharply.
	slight	decrease			decreased	slightly.

Now rewrite the sentences in B like this:

There was a slight fall in sales in Brazil.

D Practise giving information about the sales of commercial aircraft. Learner A looks at File 29 on page 119 and Learner B looks at File 30 on page 123.

A Soft drinks are big business. What do you think could make sales go up or down?

B 📼 ◎ Listen to five managers describing the sales of Fizzo. Complete the chart like this:

Area	Profit	Sales	Reasons
United Kingdom	↑	↑	
Europe			
Americas			
Australia			
Africa			

Now listen again. Why did sales go up or down?

C Study these ways of giving reasons.

Sales Profits	have	increased risen decreased fallen	**because of** **due to** **as a result of**	our new soft drink. our new factory. a price increase. the bad weather.

Match the beginning of the sentence to an end.

1 Production is more efficient …
2 Distribution is more efficient …
3 Customer service has improved …
4 Consumers have greater access to our products …
5 Our market share has increased …
6 450 employees have lost their jobs …

a … the advertising campaign.
b … new packaging methods in the factory.
c … rationalization of management structures.
d … our new centralized warehouse.
e … new vending machines on all railway stations.
f … our new distribution centre.

Then write some sentences like this:

Production is more efficient as a result of new packaging methods in the factory.

D **Find out more about the sales of soft drinks in the Americas and the Pacific Rim. Learner A looks at File 31 on page 116 and Learner B looks at File 32 on page 121.**

A You work for Marea, a small insurance company. Look at this extract from the in-company training programme. Which courses would you be interested in?

CONTENTS

1 Computing
Introduction to Windows
- Word processing
- Spreadsheets
- Database
- Presentations

2 Languages
- English
- French
- Spanish
- German
- Other

3 Telephone training

4 Personal development
- time management
- coping with stress
- effective communication

5 Induction courses for new employees

B ▭ ◉ Listen to the training manager presenting the company's new training programme to external trainers. Number these points in the order in which they are mentioned:

☐ time of change at Marea
☐ sales have increased
☐ set up in-house training programme
☐ installation of PCs
☐ identify areas for improvement
☐ increasing competition
☐ took a hard look at the way we do things

Listen again. What expressions does the speaker use to structure the presentation?

C Look at these expressions. They are useful when you have to present information.

> **Greetings**
>
> Welcome to *Marea*.
>
> **Introduction**
>
> I'm going to talk about *our new training programme*.
>
> **Beginning**
>
> I'll begin by *looking at the present system*.
> Let's start by looking at *our company's structure*.
>
> **Moving on**
>
> If we move on to *the cost of this*, …
> Let's turn to *the issue of resources*.
>
> **Concluding**
>
> To finish, *we can see that* …
> To conclude, *I suggest we do the following* …

Practise presenting information. Learner A looks at File 33 on page 119 and Learner B looks at File 34 on page 123.

D Work in small groups. You are going through your E-mail when you see this. What will you do?

> As you know, Juan has just been made a Project Manager. In this new position he has to talk to both suppliers and customers in English and is finding this very difficult. In six weeks' time, he has an important meeting with some Japanese suppliers. He has asked for some language training to help him prepare for this. What do you suggest?

Here are the alternatives. Which is the most

— flexible?
— effective?
— cost-effective?

Join an in-company extensive course (four hours per week after work).

Two-week course in an English-speaking country.

One-to-one course during work hours.

Train in the self-access centre.

What do you think the project manager should do? Present your ideas to another group.

13 Money

13.1 Negotiating the price

A Look at these situations. How are they different? In which ones can you negotiate the price?

B 📼 ◎ In addition to price, there are other matters customers can negotiate with their suppliers. Listen to this conversation and mark the things they negotiate.

quantity ☐
delivery date ☐
discount ☐
method of payment ☐
other ☐

C Study these ways of making conditions.

First conditional

If	you're prepared to wait,	we'll reduce the price.
	you take the rest,	

I'll reduce the price if you	pay cash.
	buy 1,000 pieces.

Now practise this conversation with a partner.

Ask about the price.

State price.

Reject it.

Make an offer.

Make an alternative offer.

Accept or reject it.

D Practise negotiating. Learner A looks at File 35 on page 117 and Learner B looks at File 36 on page 121.

THE FAR SIDE   By GARY LARSON

"OK. I'll go back and tell my people that you're staying in the boat, but I warn you they're *not* going to like it."

13.2 Getting paid

A Discuss these questions with a partner:

When do you pay your personal bills?

What would happen if nobody paid their bills on time?

"There. I've written all the checks for the month. I feel cleansed."

B 📼 ◎ Listen to this extract from a radio programme about payment times and complete the missing figures.

Country	Agreed time	Average time
Sweden	....	48
Denmark	30	....
Finland	....	....
UK	....	....
Italy	60	....
France	....	108

C Read this extract from a business magazine and fill in the correct headings.

a Collect your payment on time   d Keep clear and accurate records
b Set up a system   e Set out your terms of trading
c Check your customers' ability to pay

How to collect money on time
Follow these guidelines to make sure you get paid on time

.... (1)

– before you offer them credit. You may also want to check them with other businesses or ask for bank references. Make these checks at regular intervals.

.... (2)

Be specific about when you expect payment, for example, 30 days from the date of the invoice. Make sure your customer knows the terms before you do any work.

.... (3)

which enables you to issue invoices promptly and show you when invoices become overdue.

.... (4)

Incorrect invoices or unclear records are among the main reasons for delaying payment. Make sure you send invoices punctually, to the right person at the right address.

.... (5)

– install a collections routine. Keep records of all correspondence and conversations. Give priority to your largest accounts, but chase the smaller amounts too. If a customer promises you a cheque and it doesn't arrive, chase it straightaway. If regular chasing does not produce results, consider stopping further supplies to the customer. If payment is not obtained, ask a debt collector or solicitor to collect the money for you.

Reread the article and answer these questions:

6 How can you check that your customers can pay you?
7 What are some of the main reasons customers do not pay punctually?
8 What should you do if a customer does not pay on time?

Do you agree with the suggestions?

D Match a word or phrase in the text with these definitions.

a ability to buy now and pay later
b immediately
c late
d not doing something until a later time
e regular customer of a company
f sending reminders to try to get payment

A Read this letter. Why has it been written?

COTTON HOUSE
HOO FARM ESTATE, KIDDERMINSTER, WORCESTERSHIRE

Redress
The High Street
Taunton
Somerset   3 May 199-

Dear Mr Chezdoy

We regret to inform you that payment of the enclosed invoice is now 30 days overdue.

We look forward to receiving payment from you without delay.

Yours sincerely

Tara Patel

Tara Patel
Credit Controller

What information is missing from this invoice? What questions can you ask to complete it?

Invoice no. : ....
Date   : ....
Customer no. : DO 4630

Item:	No:	Units:	Price:	Total:
....	9607-52	15	£25	£375
Belts	5072-52	25	£27	£675
				£1,050

Payment within 30 days

B 🔲 ◎ Listen to Tara Patel phoning Kurt Chezdoy and complete the missing information in the invoice above.

C Study these ways of making promises.

| We'll send you a cheque | **when** / **as soon as** | we receive the goods. |

Here are some reasons for not paying an invoice.

Match the reasons to the promises below. Then make sentences like the example in the speech bubble in a.

1 ...... I find it.
2 ...... our cash flow situation improves.
3 ...... the Accounts department gets the invoice.
4 ...... you send us a corrected invoice.
5 ...... we receive a replacement.
6 ..a.. the rest of the consignment arrives.

D Practise chasing your customers for payment! Learner A looks at File 37 on page 119 and Learner B looks at File 38 on page 124.

AIMS

Discuss different countries' attitudes to gift giving
Make arrangements for a free day in a foreign city
Discuss food and its preparation

Indirect/Polite questions
Could you tell me where …?

14 Socializing

14.1 Gift-giving

A   Look at these gifts. Are they suitable for a business client in your country?

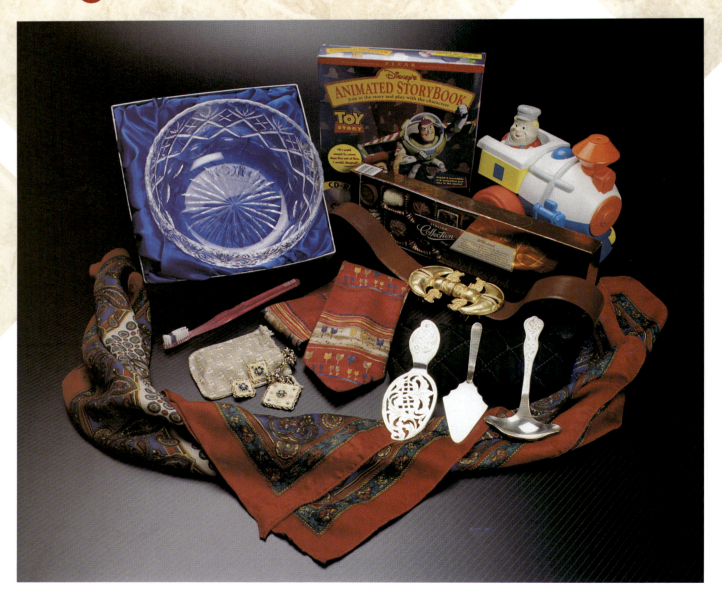

B Read this article about gift giving, then match each paragraph with one of the cultures below:

Latin America ☐   The Arab world ☐   Japan ☐

1

They give generously. If they give a lot, they expect to receive as much. Gifts for the mind such as a book or a magazine subscription are usually welcome, particularly if the choice shows a knowledge of their civilization. There are a few things to avoid: alcohol is out for Muslims; you should also be careful about items depicting animals as many mean bad luck. Bringing food or drink when you visit a home can be insulting as it may suggest that the recipient is not a good host.

2

They love giving and receiving gifts. Don't buy expensive gifts. Thoughtfulness is appreciated and cost should be secondary. If you're visiting from outside the country, bring something that is heavily taxed locally. Small electrical appliances are popular, so are scarves, perfume, candy, flowers and kitchen items. Avoid the colours of Lent – black and purple – and the unlucky number 13.

3

Personal relationships are very important. At least half the presents they give are expressions of good will. Gifts should be wrapped. If an item is unwrapped, the person may have to say they like it even if they don't. (A wrapped gift is usually opened later.) Present the gift when the recipient is alone, unless you have something for everyone in the room. Consumables and small conversation pieces such as photo books are usually welcome. Try to know the recipient's preferences because it's good to show you did your homework.

Now reread the article and answer these questions:

In which part of the world:
1 is the number 13 unlucky?
2 are animals often unlucky?
3 do people like to receive books as a gift?
4 do people like to receive food and drink as a gift?
5 is it impolite to give food and drink as a gift?
6 is it impolite to give a gift in front of other people?

C ⊟ ◎ When is a gift a bribe? Discuss these questions with a partner:

1 What is an acceptable value of a gift from a business partner?
2 Should you tell colleagues about any gifts you receive?
3 What should you do if you don't want to accept the gift?

Now listen to Maria Kelly, a business consultant, talking about gift-giving and note down her answers. Are they the same as yours?

D Discuss these questions in small groups:

Have you ever received a gift from your business partners?
When and what was it?
What did you do with it?
What gift would you like to receive from your business partners?
What gift from your country would you take abroad?
How do you feel about receiving gifts from business clients?

A You and a colleague are in Budapest on business and have a free day before you fly home. In pairs, look at this city guide and find two things you would both like to do.

Budapest at a glance

LOCATION
North/Central Hungary:
570 km Prague, 630 km Munich,
248 km Vienna

FOREIGN EXCHANGE
Open Monday to Friday, 8.30 –12.00.

ACCOMMODATION

Gellert
Tel +36 1 18 52 2000
Offers accommodation in a central location.

Hilton Hess Andras
Tel +36 1 17 51 000
Set in a breathtaking location in the old city.

EATING OUT

HUNGARIA Terez Korut
Beautiful turn-of-the-century café

Gundel
One of the city's oldest and best eateries

SHOPPING

Vaci Utca
Offers everything from exclusive boutiques to market stalls.

Nagykorsi
Monday to Saturday 8.00–15.00 h.
A market with a wide range of goods at a wide range of prices.

TRANSPORT
Tram, bus and metro cost 19 Hungarian florins for a daily ticket available from metro stations.

TELEPHONING
Country code 36, Area code 1

AN HOUR TO SPARE?
Take to the streets. Visit the city's best preserved Turkish baths, *Kiraly furdo*. Walk around the beautiful old city.

ENTERTAINMENT
Budapest offers a variety of cultural activities. For opera fans there are the splendid State Opera and the *Erkel*. For classical music, try the Academy of Music (*Zeakademia*) and the spectacular mid-19th century Vigado concert hall.

TRADE FAIRS AND EXHIBITIONS
Open air performances on Margaret Island from June; Hungarian Grand Prix (at Hungoring) in August. Arts Week in September includes concerts, theatre, dance and art exhibitions, continuing into October.

B Here are some questions about Budapest. What are the answers?

Could you tell me the best way to get about town?

Do you know what time Nagykorsi market closes?

Could you tell me the phone number of the Gellert Hotel?

Do you know when the Arts Week is?

Could you tell me where I can change money?

C Study these ways of asking polite questions.

> **Wh- questions with to be**
>
> What**'s** the best way to get around town?
>
> **Indirect questions with to be**
>
> Could you tell me
> Do you know | what the best way to get around town **is**?

> **Wh- questions with do/does/did**
>
> What time **does** Nagykorsi market **close**?
>
> **Indirect questions with do/does/did**
>
> **Could** you tell me
> **Do** you know | what time Nagykorsi market **closes**?

Here are the answers to some more questions. What are the questions?

1 36	4 Twelve o'clock.
2 17 51 000	5 HUF 19.
3 In August.	6 Monday to Saturday, from eight o'clock to three o'clock. 6

Practise asking and answering these questions with a partner. Then change partners and answer the same questions about a city you know.

D Work in small groups. Look at the headings in **A** again. Make a similar guide about the place you're learning English in.

A   Discuss these questions with a partner:

What time do you arrange a business lunch for?
How long does it last?
Do you discuss business during the meal? If so, when?

B   🔲 ◎ Listen to a woman talking about a business lunch she went to in Spain.

What time was the lunch?
How long did it last?
Did they discuss business during the meal?

C Look at this menu. What would you like to eat?

MENU

PEPPERS BRASSERIE

Cream of spinach soup with smoked bacon and croutons
Fried camembert with a winter berry compote
Mixed salad

Roast pheasant with redcurrant and blackcurrant jelly
Grilled Scottish salmon with champagne hollandaise
Crespolini pancake with ratatouille, cream cheese and spinach
Puree of three root vegetables
Brussels sprouts with nut butter
Roast and boiled potatoes

Bitter-sweet chocolate cake with chocolate sauce and cream
Mature Stilton with oat biscuits

Coffee with chocolates

£23.95 per person, inc. VAT
12.5 per cent service charge

For reservations please phone 600 1111

Look at the menu again. How many different ways of cooking food can you find?

D What are some specialities from your region or country? Explain them to a partner. You can use these expressions to help you:

… is a local speciality.
It's made with …
It's served with …
It's quite spicy/mild/rich.
I (don't) think you'd like it.

15 Revision and consolidation

A Grammar Correct the mistakes in these sentences.

a This is the catalogue who we send to all our new customers.
b Mr Saloman is the sales representative which is responsible for Malaysia.
c There was a slightly decline in sales in Eastern Europe.
d This was because the poor exchange rate.
e In North America, sales rose dramatic.
f This large increase in sales was mainly due new products.
g If you'll take 30, we'll give you a 15 per cent discount.
h I take 30 if you deliver before the end of the month.
i We'll give you another 3 per cent discount when you pay cash.
j We'll write you a cheque if you send us the invoice.
k Can you tell me where is the nearest Metro station?
l Do you know what time do the banks open?

B What do you say? Match the function to the actual words.

1 Give reasons for something.
2 Apologize.
3 Ask about prices.
4 Ask a guest about their food.
5 Structure a talk.
6 Thank someone for a gift.
7 Accept a deal.
8 Describe food.

a That's fine.
b Thank you very much. That's lovely.
c How's the fish?
d It's a result of the poor summer.
e It's quite spicy.
f I'm afraid we've got cash flow problems at the moment.
g What price do you have in mind?
h First we'll look at last year's sales.

Now write a short dialogue using some of these phrases.

C Vocabulary Look at these categories. How many words can you put in each category?

Promotional items   Describing trends   Food flavours

D **Reading** What do people in your country wear to work? What are office hours in your country? What are banking hours in your country? Now read this article and find out about business practice in Malaysia.

Business hints

Smart, light-weight clothing is ideal for doing business. For men, a tie and long-sleeved shirt is usual for most work encounters. A jacket is required for top level meetings and 5-star functions.

Although punctuality is expected, Malaysians will understand if you are trapped in a traffic jam on your way to a meeting. Malaysians are generally polite, considerate and tolerant.

Carry plenty of business cards. As a sign of respect, present your card with both hands, or with your left hand resting lightly on your right forearm.

Normal office hours are 9.00 to 17.00, while banking hours are 10.00 to 15.00 Monday to Friday and 9.30 to 11.30 on Saturday. Most people start work early and can most easily be reached in the morning.

In recognition of the Islamic majority, whose day of worship is Friday, many people extend Friday lunchtime (12.00–15.00) or leave work early. Friday is not a good time to travel or get someone's full attention.

Reread the article and correct these statements.

1 Men should always wear a jacket and tie to work.
2 It's not important to be punctual.
3 You should present your business card with your right hand.
4 Office hours are from 10.00 to 15.00.
5 Banks are not open on Saturday.
6 The best time to contact people is early afternoon.

E **Listening** Listen to a conversation about transport in Kuala Lumpur. How many different forms of transport do the speakers mention? Which one do they recommend?

Listen again. The speakers talk about transport costs in the Malaysian currency, Ringgits (RM) and sen. Write down the answers to the following:

1 Taxi from airport to downtown ....
2 Surcharge for taxis from a hotel ....
3 Surcharge for taxis after midnight ....
4 Minibuses ....
5 Car hire per day ....
6 Petrol per litre ....

Relative clauses

Who/that = people (not things)
A customer is someone **who** buys something from a company.

Which/that = things
An invoice is something **which** asks for payment of goods or services.

Adjectives and adverbs

In Europe, there was a **sharp** increase in sales.
In other markets, sales decreased **slightly**.

Cause and result

Sales have risen **because of** our new soft drink.
Profits have decreased **due to** price increases.
Sales have fallen **as a result of** the poor weather.

First conditional

If you **take** the rest, we**'ll reduce** the price.	I**'ll give** you a discount **if** you **pay** cash.
If you **don't take** the rest, we **won't reduce** the price.	I **won't give** you a discount **if** you **don't pay** cash.

If, **when**, **as soon as** are usually followed by the present simple.

N.B. If: it's possible something will happen.
We'll give you a discount **if** you pay within seven days.
When: it's certain something will happen
We'll send you a cheque **when** we receive the goods.

Polite questions

Questions with *to be*
What **is** the best way to the hotel?   Do you know what the best way to the hotel **is**?
Where **is** the market?   Could you tell me where the market **is**?

Questions with *do/does/did*
When **does** the market **close**?   **Do** you know what time the market **closes**?
How much **does** a tram ticket **cost**?   **Could** you tell me how much a tram ticket **costs**?

Useful words and expressions

Your translation

advertising ....
direct mail ....

dramatic ....
gradual ....
sharp ....
slight ....
sudden ....
steady ....

negotiate ....
quantity ....
delivery ....
method of payment ....
discount ....

invoice ....
overdue ....
reminder ....

Giving a talk
Welcome to … ....
I'm going to talk about … ....
I'll begin by … ....
Let's start by looking at … ....
Let's turn to … ....
To finish, … ....
To conclude, … ....

Talking about food
… is a local speciality. ....
It's made with … ....
It's served with … ....
It's quite spicy/mild/rich. ....
I (don't) think you'd like it. ....

Correspondence
We enclose *our order form.* ....
Please confirm *delivery in six weeks.* ....
We look forward to *receiving the goods.* ....
We would like to place an order. ....

You might also find it helpful to make lists of the following vocabulary: promotional items your company uses, ways to promote a product, verbs to describe an upward movement, verbs to describe a downward movement, and your favourite food.

AIMS

Discuss a company's culture
Express probability
Give an opinion
Express preference

Modal verbs
would/might/wouldn't

16 Business culture and ethics

16.1 Corporate culture

A Look at this photograph. Would you like to work here?

B Read these texts about three different companies. In which company do:

a staff use first names? ....

b managers have their own car park? ....

c managers and workers wear the same clothes? ....

d managers have their own dining room? ....

e staff sit together in one office? ....

f workers get gold stars for good performance? ....

88

At the **600 group**, a British-owned manufacturer of lathes, managers have their own dining room and car park. It does not matter 'two hoots', says Anthony Sweeten, the Managing Director, that workers and managers lunch and park separately. Workers used to be rewarded for 25 years' service with an invitation to lunch in the executive dining room. But they never accepted. This shows, says Mr Sweeten, that his employees are not interested in integrating with management. They find management issues boring. 'They don't want to be responsible for too much. They want management to manage.'

Many workers at the 600 group say that managers ask for their ideas but do not listen to their suggestions. So they have stopped making them.

Bosch is a German car-component company with a factory in Wales.

Workers talk enthusiastically about the products they make. One worker says that in previous jobs he used to change out of work clothes as soon as his shift was over. Now he enjoys walking through town in his Bosch overalls.

Bosch workers and managers clock in and out together, wear the same overalls, share all facilities. Workers are described as team members. There are few complaints from the shop floor that managers ignore their suggestions. The problem at Bosch is dealing with the number of ideas. In place of the division between the shop floor and the offices, divisions have opened on the shop floor itself. Shifts compete to better each other's output. Some shifts have even been accused of holding up uninteresting tasks to slow down their competitors on later shifts.

At **First Direct** everyone uses first names.

Staff organize themselves into teams; good performance means gold stars. Part of the First Direct culture is that all staff, whether chief executive or chief receptionist, sit together; well, not all at the same desk but almost. To stress the one-level egalitarian structure, the bank is situated in a one-level warehouse. Upstairs has no meaning; there is no executive floor or even washroom. The Chief Executive Officer keeps a careful eye on customer service: the staff all sit together, but Little Brother is certainly watching them. On his way home, he does not relax; he plays taped recordings on his car cassette of his staff on the telephone.

Which companies would you like to work for? Why?

C Match a word in the text with these definitions:

600 group
a a machine used to shape wood or metal
b a canteen for senior employees
c the people who make and carry out decisions in the company

Bosch
d past or former
e working clothes
f to record the time you start and finish work
g assembly line workers in a factory

First Direct
h the workers or employees of an organization
i an organization in which all people are equal
j a building to store raw materials or finished goods

D Find out about another learner's company. You can ask questions like these:

Do you use first names or surnames at work?
Where do the managers eat?
Do you get anything for 25 years' service?

Do you work together in teams?
Do you all sit in one office?
Does management listen to the workers?

A These people are job-hunting. Look at what they say. Do you agree with them?

I definitely wouldn't work for a company with a bad safety record.

I might work for a company with a history of environmental accidents.

I probably wouldn't work for a cigarette manufacturer.

I'd work for a company that makes weapons.

B Look at these ways of expressing probability.

100% ↓	I would I'd definitely		
75% ↓	I'd probably		
50% ↓	I might Perhaps I would	work for	an arms dealer. a bank. the government. a political pressure group.
25% ↓	I probably wouldn't		
0%	I wouldn't I definitely wouldn't		

Which companies would you work or not work for? Ask some other learners.

C Do this quiz.

WHAT ARE YOUR personal standards?

1 A colleague obtains a confidential report from a competitor. It contains information important to your sales effort. Would you read it and use it?

Definitely ☐ Probably ☐
Possibly ☐ Definitely not ☐

2 You have to pick up your child from school early even though you have an important meeting at work. This has happened four times in the past month. Would you tell your boss the truth?

Definitely ☐ Probably ☐
Possibly ☐ Definitely not ☐

3 You've been working late and on weekends. Recently you had lunch with an old friend and picked up the tab. When the bill comes, would you put it on your next expense account?

Definitely ☐ Probably ☐
Possibly ☐ Definitely not ☐

4 Do you think the following are a serious problem (1), a minor problem (2) or not an ethical problem (3) at work?

	1	2	3
Taking office supplies home	☐	☐	☐
Copying computer software for personal use	☐	☐	☐
Making personal calls on the company phone	☐	☐	☐
Calling in sick when you need a day off	☐	☐	☐
Sharing company discounts with a friend	☐	☐	☐
Padding expense accounts	☐	☐	☐

D Compare your answers to the quiz with some other learners.

16.3 A woman's place

A Look at these job categories. Which category do *secretary* and *nanny* come under?

a clerical
b government administration and managerial
c personal, catering and security services
d production, transport and construction
e professional and technical
f sales workers and managers
g agricultural

Now think of two jobs for each category.

B This chart shows the percentage of women (as opposed to men) working in these job areas in the European Union. Which job categories from **A** do you think they refer to? Mark them on the chart.

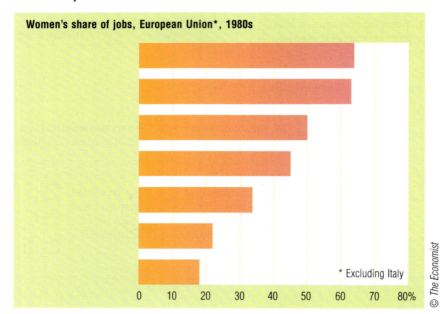

Women's share of jobs, European Union*, 1980s

* Excluding Italy

© *The Economist*

Now look at File 41 on page 118 and see if you are right!

C Look at these statements. Do you think they are true (T) or false (F)?

		You	Radio programme
a	The number of women in work has increased.	☐	☐
b	The number of men in work has decreased.	☐	☐
c	Most women with children do not go out to work.	☐	☐
d	It is difficult for women to find work.	☐	☐
e	Men and women usually do the same jobs.	☐	☐
f	The number of part-time jobs is increasing.	☐	☐

🔊 ◎ Now listen to this extract from a radio programme and see if you are right.

D Look at these ways of expressing an opinion.

100%	I'm sure …
↓	I'm certain …
75%	I expect …
↓	It's likely …
50%	I might …
↓	Perhaps …
25%	I don't expect …
↓	It's unlikely …
0%	I'm sure …
	I'm certain + not …

What do you think? Complete these sentences so they express your opinion.

In ten years' time:

a .... most women will work part-time.

b .... more men will work part-time.

c .... women will earn the same as men.

d .... there will be more women managers.

e .... the situation of women at work will have changed greatly.

Compare your opinions with some other learners.

AIMS

Discuss green issues in the office
Make recommendations
Ask for an opinion and agree or disagree

Reported speech
Reporting verbs

17 Meetings

17.1 Greening the office

A **Look at these suggestions for greening the office. Does your company do any of these things?**

- [ ] Writes to customers on recycled paper.
- [ ] Uses china cups instead of plastic ones.
- [ ] Encourages employees to cycle to work.
- [ ] Bans smoking in the company.
- [ ] Sorts rubbish.
- [ ] Uses refillable ink pens instead of disposable ones.

B 📼 ◎ Listen to two people talking about the above proposals for greening their place of work. Is the second speaker for (F) or against (A) these proposals?

Proposal	F/A	Reason
1		
2		
3		
4		
5		
6		

Listen again and make notes on the reasons the second speaker gives.

C Study these ways of taking part in a discussion.

> **Making recommendations**
>
> I (don't) think we should use refillable pens.
> In my opinion we ought to use recycled paper.
> I suggest cycling to work.
>
> **Asking for opinions**
>
> What do you think about driving to work?
> How do you feel about this?
>
> **Agreeing and disagreeing**
>
> That's a good idea.
> I agree with you.
> I don't think that's a very good idea.
> I'm afraid I don't agree.

Work with a partner and practise making recommendations about the topics in **A** like this.

I think we should write to customers on recycled paper. What do you think?

That's a good idea. It would also save a lot of money.

I'm afraid I don't agree. It would be bad for our image.

D You are going to green your office or school. Work in small groups and decide what you are going to do.

A Evergreen, a cosmetics company, is going to launch a new bath oil. Read these minutes from a recent meeting held to discuss the packaging of the bath oil. What do you think the people actually said? For example, James: *I think we should use plastic bottles.*

MINUTES OF MEETING

Present: James, Laura, Max, Nic, Olivia

1 Apologies for absence – Ali, Mary

2 The minutes of the last meeting were agreed on.

3 Packaging of *Black Musk* bath oil

James recommended using plastic bottles because they are light, easy to pack and easy to transport. Furthermore, they do not break.

Olivia suggested glass bottles would give the bath oil a more upmarket image.

Max pointed out that glass is easier to recycle than plastic. James wondered if customers would actually bring bottles back for refilling.

Laura pointed out that if we use glass we will need to find a new supplier as our present supplier only deals in plastics. She agreed to get quotes from different suppliers in time for the next meeting.

4 Any other business – none

The next meeting will be on 15 March at 10.00.

B Now listen to a recording made at the meeting. Compare what you think the speakers said with their actual words.

C Look at these verbs. They are used to report what people say.

Reporting statements

He	said explained pointed out told him	that plastic bottles are easy to use.

Reporting suggestions

She	suggested recommended	using glass bottles.

Reporting commands

She | **told** him | to get a quote from some suppliers.

Match what people said to how it is reported.

1 Why don't we use coloured glass?
2 Could you find out the prices for blue and green glass?
3 I don't think that's a very good idea. You can't see what's in the bottles.
4 Would it be more expensive?
5 We could have different colours for different lines.
6 I think we should use glass.

a She asked him to find out the prices for different colours.
b He recommended using glass.
c He wondered if it would be more expensive.
d She suggested using coloured glass.
e She said we could have different colours for different lines.
f He disagreed.

D Evergreen is also thinking of introducing a refill system for its haircare products. Learner A looks at File 42 on page 122 and Learner B looks at File 43 on page 120.

17.3 Cutting costs

A You are a senior manager at Phoenix, a small advertising company. Last year the company overspent in the following areas. Can you think of any ways of cutting costs?

Item	Overspend
Marketing	
Entertaining clients	£10,500
Promotional gifts	£8,500
Overheads	
Cleaning	£8,500
Heating	£20,000
Sales	
Hotel accommodation	£22,500
Travel expenses	£20,000
Staff benefits	
Company car for managers	£50,000
Ten year service bonus	£8,500

B Study these expressions used in discussions.

Starting

Let's start.
As you know, we're here to discuss …

Interrupting

Sorry, can I just say something?
Sorry to interrupt, but …

Dealing with interruptions

Can I just finish?
Just a minute, …

Moving on

Can we move on to the next point?

Keeping to the point

Let's not get sidetracked.
Can we keep to the point?

Finishing

So, can we all agree that …
OK. To sum up so far …

C Work in groups. You are going to hold a meeting to find ways of saving money at Phoenix. Learner A looks at File 44 on page 119 and Learner B looks at File 45 on page 122. Learner C looks at File 46 on page 124 and Learner D looks at File 47 on page 116.

Make sure you have a chair to lead the discussion and a secretary to take the minutes.

D Now write up the minutes of your meeting. When you have finished, show them to another group.

AIMS

Describe a process
Describe a company's history

Modals
have to/must/can/don't have to/can't/mustn't

Passive
past and present

18 Processes

18.1 Talking about regulations

A Discuss these questions with a partner. Use the words in the box below to help you.

What hours do people work in your company?
Do all departments work the same hours?
What do you personally like or dislike about your   working hours?

flexitime   core time   breaks   overtime   shifts   free time

B Listen to Rita Marques talking about working times at her company to a colleague from another country. Are these statements true (T) or false (F)?

Employees:
1 have to work 40 hours a week.
2 can't start work at 7 a.m.
3 don't have to clock off for coffee breaks.
4 must not do overtime.
5 can take three days a month of free time.
6 don't have to work shifts.

100

C Study these ways of talking about obligation and possibility.

| We | have to / must | work 140 hours a month. |

We **can** start work at 7 a.m.

We **don't have to** clock off for coffee breaks.

We **can't** finish work before 4 p.m.

We **mustn't** smoke in the office.

Find out something about some other learners' working hours. Use this table to help you.

Do you have to:	Learner 1	Learner 2	Learner 3	Learner 4
start work before 8 a.m.?				
work on Friday afternoons?				
do a lot of overtime?				
work shifts?				
take your holiday in summer?				
??? (make a question of your own)				

D Work in small groups. You work for Canine Candies, a small company which produces gift confectionery for dog-lovers. Your task is to draw up regulations for workers in the production area. Use these ideas to help you:

Working hours   Holidays   Clothing   Safety

A Look at this car. Can you name the various parts?

1 Underbody
2 Roof
3 Front wing
4 Body
5 Engine
6 Wheels
7 Gearbox
8 Headlights

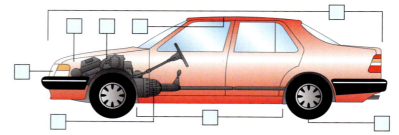

B This diagram shows the production process in a modern car plant. Match each text to the right part of the diagram.

a Headlights are adjusted before final inspection and the car is driven away.
b Doors are removed to prevent damage when the glass and other parts are fitted.
c The top coats of paint are applied and baked on.
d Doors, front wings and other parts are fitted before inspection.
e Engine, gearbox, seats and wheels are added. Doors rejoin the same car they were removed from.
f Parts are delivered. The underbody and side panels are assembled with the aid of robots.
g The car body is dipped in a protective undercoat and then baked to harden the paint.
h Roof sections are added and panels are welded together by robot.

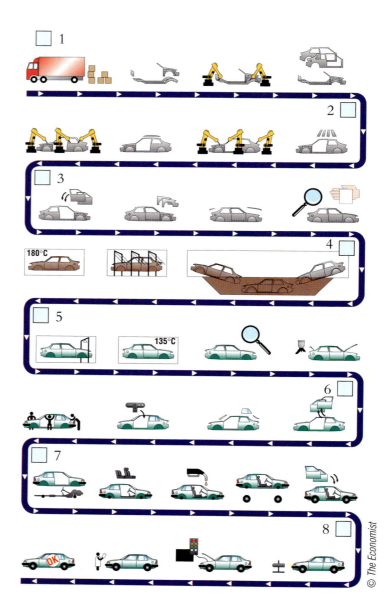

C Study the passive form.

> The body **is painted**.
> The side panels **are assembled**.
> The doors **are fitted**.
> The headlights **are adjusted**.

Look at this cartoon of a 'typical' American car. Make some sentences like this: *The gasoline is refined from Persian Gulf oil.* Use the words in the box to help you.

> to manufacture   to build   to make   to produce   to assemble   to refine

D Make notes on a process you know. Then explain it to a partner. Use these words to help you.

First, …
Next, …
Then, …
After that, …
Finally, …

A 📼 ◎ Listen to someone giving a talk on the history of Hershey, the American chocolate manufacturer. Fill in the missing dates.

The Hershey headquarters, 1905 – 1935

The Hershey headquarters, 1935 – 1968

Milton S. Hershey

1 Lancaster Caramel Company founded

....

2 Lancaster Caramel Company sold

....

3 New Hershey's factory completed

....

4 Village renamed

....

5 Hershey's Kisses

....

6 Mr Goodbar

....

7 Listed on New York Stock Exchange

....

A packaging label from the 1920s

The House 🔲 of Hershey
Where Quality is Paramount

Chocolate Avenue, Hershey, Pennsylvania

B Study the past form of the passive.

> The Lancaster Caramel company **was founded** in 1886.
> The new Hershey's chocolate factory **was completed** in 1905.
> *Hershey's Kisses* **were** first **manufactured** in 1907.

Now make some sentences about the history of Hershey. Use the information in **A** and the verbs in the box to help you.

> introduce   manufacture   list   found   complete   rename   sell

C Look at this fact sheet for *Hershey's Kisses*. Use the facts to produce an information sheet for your customers. You can start like this:

> *Hershey's Kisses* chocolates, a little product with a big future, were first introduced in 1907.

Hershey's Kisses
chocolates fact sheet

KEY DATES

1907	*Hershey's Kisses* chocolates first introduced.
1907 to 1921	*Hershey's Kisses* wrapped by hand.
August 1921	*Hershey's Kisses* wrapping machines first used.
August 1921	Flag added to *Hershey's Kisses* chocolates.
1942 to 1949	Production of *Hershey's Kisses* stopped due to rationing of silver foil during World War II.
1962	*Hershey's Kisses* packaged in colors other than silver for the first time. Red, green and silver produced for the Christmas season.
1990	*Hershey's Kisses with Almonds* chocolates launched nationally.
1993	*Hugs* and *Hugs with Almonds* launched nationally.

Hershey's Kisses
chocolates fact sheet

D Make notes on the history of a company you know: its founder, the history of different products, buildings, etc. Take another learner on a tour of this company and tell them something about it.

AIMS

Get information about hotels
Organize a conference
Give a brief presentation

19 Conferences

19.1 Finding a location

A You work for KEF, a company which produces top-of-the-range loudspeakers. Part of your job is to help arrange the annual sales conference. This year it will be somewhere in Switzerland. You expect about 40 overseas distributors to attend.

First, look at the *To do* list and decide which order you should do these things in.

To do

☐ Arrange accommodation for participants.
☐ Prepare conference folders.
☐ Book venue.
☐ Draw up conference schedule.
☐ Send out invitations to participants.

☐ Decide on social programme.
☐ Set dates for conference.
☐ Finalize conference schedule.
☐ Find a suitable conference venue.
☐ Send joining instructions to participants.

B Here are some things you need to know before you choose a venue for the conference.

Where exactly is the venue?
What is the nearest airport? How long does it take to get there?
What kind of accommodation is available?
Are there restaurants nearby? What kind of food do they offer?
Is there any kind of entertainment?
What conference facilities are available?
Other information?

Now read these entries from a hotel guide and find answers to the questions above.

Arosa Kulm Hotel

The Kulm is one of the oldest and best established hotels in Arosa. A two-hour drive or three-hour train journey away from Zurich airport, it enjoys an absolutely prime location at the end of the village, overlooking the sunny south side. During winter the funiculars and skilifts carry you to the *pistes*, most of which lead straight back to the Kulm. The Weisshornbahn and Hörnli Express take you to the starting points of grand hikes during the summer.

The Kulm offers 44 single rooms, 92 double rooms, and 10 apartments, all fully equipped to the highest standards.

In-hotel dining facilities include the hotel restaurant and a number of speciality restaurants. There are also several bars, including the popular poolside bar.

The Arosa Kulm hotel is fully equipped for conferences of up to 80 people. Details available on request.

Le Montreux Palace

Beautifully situated on the shores of Lake Geneva, the hotel is accessible from Geneva's Cointrin airport by train in 70 minutes or by taxi in 45 minutes. The International Convention Centre in Montreux is 3 minutes on foot.

This magnificent hotel features a fully preserved Art Nouveau heritage and offers 240 elegant rooms, two restaurants, two bars and a casino for its demanding clientele. Medieval candlelit dinners can be arranged at the Oron Castle, which is operated by the hotel.

As the most prestigious and traditional hotel in the Lake Geneva area, Le Montreux Palace can handle any event, from a meeting for 20 to a congress for 1,400 persons. Twelve meeting rooms are available for congresses and conferences, presentations, banquets, fashion shows and exhibitions, including all the technical equipment you need.

Which hotel would you prefer? Why?

C Find out more about conference facilities at Le Montreux Palace. Learner A looks at File 48 on page 121 and Learner B looks at File 49 on page 124.

D Use these notes to write to the Arosa Kulm Hotel to request similar information.

Sales conference: 29 June – 1 July
- 1 Meeting room for 40 people (needs excellent acoustics to demonstrate new products)
- OHP, flipchart, video
- Rooms for 40 people, preferably single
- Prices?

19.2 Organizing the conference

 A You have arranged a venue for the annual sales conference. You must now draw up a schedule for the three days. You should include these things:

- Discussion of last year's sales results (one morning or afternoon)
- Medieval dinner at Oron Castle (one evening)
- Presentation of new range (one morning or afternoon)
- Hiking in Alps (one morning or afternoon)
- Welcome by company Chair (30 minutes)
- Discussion of new promotion campaign (one morning or afternoon)

What other items might be on a conference schedule?

	29 June	30 June	1 July
9.00			
11.00	Coffee	Coffee	Coffee
11.30			
13.00	Lunch	Lunch	Lunch
14.00			
16.00	Coffee	Coffee	Coffee
16.30			
18.30	Dinner	Dinner	Dinner

B Add the punctuation to this letter inviting one of your distributors to the conference.

KEF Audio

MAIDSTONE KENT ME15 6QP
Tel: (01622) 672261
Fax: (01622) 750653

yoshi watenabe
2-9-9 shinjuku, shinjuku-ku
toyko 160
japan

23 february 199-

dear yoshi

we would like to invite you to join us for the annual sales conference and launch of the new KEF loudspeaker range at montreux switzerland from 29 june to 1 july we enclose brochures on our new range together with a conference programme please let us know if you wish to attend as soon as possible

best wishes

C You have now sent out the letters of invitation. Read these E-mails and decide what the problems are.

1
```
Could you let me know who pays for accommodation and travel
to and from the conference?
Regards
Jan Zednik
```

2
```
Will there be vegetarian food available?
Looking forward to seeing you again at the conference.
Regards
Susie Tan
```

🔊 ◎ You've asked several colleagues for information to help you solve these problems. Match the voice-mail with the E-mail messages above.

Message 1:   Message 2:

D Draft E-mails or send voice-mail replies to the people above.

19.3 Presenting your product

A Your task is to prepare a presentation for the Sales Conference. Before you start, discuss these questions in small groups.

Have you ever attended a presentation?
What was good? What was not so good?
Have you ever made a presentation?
What was the most difficult thing?

B Look at this brochure for the new range of KEF loudspeakers. Do you think they are attractive?

KEF: Quality and excellence since 1961 ...

In 1961 Raymond Cooke founded KEF in a hut at a metalworking operation called Kent Engineering and Foundry (KEF). From these small beginnings, KEF has grown to become one of the most important designers and manufacturers of loudspeakers in the world. Yet KEF today still operates out of its original site at Maidstone, England.

From the beginning the company placed great emphasis on engineering, producing unusual speakers that made full use of new materials and technology. The company's first speaker, the K1, was an immediate success, and the huge sales of the next model, the Celeste, ensured the long-term future of the company.

In 1967, as a result of experiments with new materials, KEF developed a new range of loudspeaker parts. These used a lightweight plastic that was flexible and yet held its shape. Many millions of these units have been sold, and some versions of this design are still in production today.

The Celeste speaker

In 1973 KEF was the first speaker company to use computer assisted design: this allowed engineers and designers to vastly improve the sound quality of its products. In that same year, KEF introduced the Reference Series of speakers, which was widely praised. In 1975 three new series of speakers were designed, and the company won more awards for excellence.

Combining the newest of materials and techniques with traditional crafts skills has earned the company one of the finest reputations in the industry. Over the years, KEF loudspeakers have been praised by critics world-wide and also won numerous awards. With their life-like sound, excellent performance and beautiful design, KEF loudspeakers are more than high-fidelity. They are music.

The latest from the greatest: The RDM Two loudspeaker

Engineered to deliver the clearest, most truthful sound, these speakers use the latest technology to bring your music to life. Attractive bookshelf size speakers that will enhance your home as well as your listening.

Weight: 8.3 kg
Size (H x W x D): 330 x 234 x 250 mm
Individually crafted to the highest standards

The RDM Two speaker

110

Read through the brochure in detail and answer these questions.

1 Who started the company?
2 Was the first speaker successful?
3 What did KEF start using in 1973?
4 What features make KEF so successful?
5 What dimensions are the new speakers?

C Work in small groups. Using the information from the brochure and your own ideas, prepare a short presentation on KEF's new range of loudspeakers. You should cover the following points:

- Welcome your audience
- Introduce yourself
- Give an overview of the history of the company and its first products
- Describe this year's new products, comparing them with earlier products
- Thank your audience for coming.

You can start like this:

Welcome to KEF's annual sales conference. I'm Pauline and today I'm going to talk about …

And finish like this:

Thank you for coming. I hope I've shown you some ways you can increase your sales in the coming year and I look forward to seeing you again at next year's conference.

D Work in small groups. Listen to other learners' presentations.

20 Revision and consolidation

A **Grammar** Correct the mistakes in these sentences.

a I had definitely not make personal calls from the office.
b Probably I wouldn't send personal letters by my E-mail.
c I expect not that prices will go up next year.
d Mr Tanaka said me that he's not satisfied with our present supplier.
e He suggested to look for a new one.
f I told him I agree not with that.
g He asked me that I get some quotes.
h Most of our output is export to Central Europe.
i Some of our models are also selled in the States.
j This factory was complete five years ago.
k Last year over 200,000 cars produced here.

B **What do you say?** Match the function to the actual words.

1 Ask someone for their opinion.
2 Disagree with someone.
3 Say something is probable.
4 Make a recommendation.
5 Say something is not probable.
6 Deal with an interruption.
7 Say something is necessary.
8 Interrupt someone.

a I'm afraid I don't think that's a very good idea.
b We have to find ways of increasing sales.
c I don't think we should do that.
d Sorry, can I just say something?
e It's unlikely that customers will want a more expensive model.
f We might be able to produce it in different colours.
g Sorry, can I just finish?
h What do you think about that?

C **Vocabulary** Put these words into four categories and then give them a heading.

OHP   first   engine   wing   then   add   assemble   finally   flipchart   fit   video   body

Add some more words to each category.

112

D 🔊 ◎ **Listening** This chart shows how cars are made in three different continents. Listen and complete the information on Japan and Europe.

Three approaches to car making	Japan	USA	Europe
Performance			
Productivity (hours per car)	....	25.1	....
Quality (defects per 100 cars)	....	82	....
Employees			
Workforce in teams (per cent)	....	17.3	....
Suggestions (per employee per year)	....	0.4	....
Number of job classifications	....	67	....
Training of new workers (hours)	....	46	....
Automation (percentage of process automated)			
Welding	....	76	....
Painting	....	34	....
Assembly	....	1	....

© The Economist

Now answer these questions.

Where are: the best trained workers?   the lowest number of different jobs?
the highest number of teams?

E **Reading** Read this article about total productive maintenance in the Pirelli factory in Carlisle and answer these questions:

What does the factory make?   What award did it win?   How did it achieve this?

Japanese standards? *No problem*

Quality gurus laughed when Pirelli's tyre factory in Carlisle took up the challenge of Total Productive Maintenance (TPM) and set itself a three-year target to win Japan's top industrial efficiency award. Implementing the programme was painful, but last November the factory won the Japanese Institute of Plant Maintenance's TPM award. It is the first in England to earn the certification.

Carlisle is now a benchmark of manufacturing excellence within the Pirelli empire and regularly receives best-practice visits from other multinationals. It specializes in high-performance tyres for Jaguar and BMW as well as supplying other manufacturers. It exports 55 per cent of its output.

TPM has had a significant effect on the factory's manufacturing culture. Output has increased by 45 per cent, productivity by 20 per cent and training time by 200 per cent. A programme of preventive maintenance has drastically reduced machinery breakdowns. For the key machines, where failure can result in production loss, the breakdown rate is now only 4 per cent of what it was.

The system of grouping workers encourages worker-participation by inviting ideas on how processes can be improved. Some 6,000 – 8,000 are put forward each year.

© Telegraph Group Lttd. London 1996

Now reread the article and match a percentage to what they refer to.

1	4 per cent	a	increase in training time
2	20 per cent	b	increase in output
3	45 per cent	c	output for export
4	55 per cent	d	increase in productivity
5	200 per cent	e	present breakdown rate

Summary

Expressing probability

100%	I would/I'd definitely …
75%	I'd probably …
50%	I might/Perhaps I would …
25%	I probably wouldn't …
0%	I wouldn't/I definitely wouldn't …

I'd **probably** work for a bank.
I **might** work for the government.
I **definitely wouldn't** work for an arms dealer.

Expressing opinions

100%	I'm sure/I'm certain …
75%	I expect/It's likely …
50%	I might/Perhaps …
25%	I don't expect/It's unlikely …
0%	I'm sure/I'm certain + not …

I expect **I'll** stay with this company.
It's unlikely that **I'll get** a full-time job.
I'm sure my next boss **won't** be a woman.

Reporting what people say

Reporting statements

She **said** plastic bottles are easier to transport.
He **pointed out** they are more difficult to recycle.
She **told us** we will need a new supplier.

Reporting suggestions

He **recommended using** glass bottles.

Reporting commands

She **asked** him **to** get a quote from some suppliers.

Passive

Present simple

It **is**	(not) **made** in Korea.	**Is** it	**made** in Korea?	Yes, it **is**.
They **are**		**Are** they		No, they **aren't**.

The body **is painted** in this factory.
The doors **are not fitted** by robots.
Are the tyres **made** in the USA? Yes, they **are**.

Past simple

It **was**	(not) **launched**.	**Was** it	**launched**?	Yes, it **was**.
They **were**		**Were** they		No, they **weren't**.

The company **was founded** in 1897.
When **was** the factory **built**?

Useful words and expressions

Your translation

definitely ....
probably ....
possibly ....

office supplies ....
expense account ....

explain ....
point out ....
recommend ....
suggest ....
wonder ....

recycle *a product* ....
refill *a bottle* ....
overheads ....

minutes of a meeting ....
apologies for absence ....
any other business ....

apply *a coat of paint* ....
adjust *the headlights* ....
assemble *the parts* ....
remove *the doors* ....
fit *the wings* ....
weld *the panels* ....

found a company ....
build a factory ....
introduce a product ....
manufacture a product ....

Making recommendations
I (don't) think we should …
In my opinion we ought to … ....
I suggest *verb+ing* … ....

Asking for opinions
What do you think about *verb+ing*? ....
How do you feel about this? ....

Agreeing
That's a good idea.
I agree with you. ....

Disagreeing
I don't think that's a very good idea. ....
I'm afraid I don't agree. ....

Interrupting
Sorry, can I just say something? ....
Sorry to interrupt, but … ....

Dealing with interruptions
Can I just finish? ....
Just a minute, … ....

Files

File 47

STAFF BENEFITS

Your task is to find ways of cutting staff benefits. This is the situation at present:

- All managers have a company car: at the moment this is a Mercedes.
- Bonus for ten years' service: 2 months' extra salary.

File 39

You are Pierre Lecerf.

Today's date is 7 October. You will get a phone call about this invoice.

COTTON HOUSE
HOO FARM ESTATE, KIDDERMINSTER, WORCESTERSHIRE

Pierre Lecerf
Rue de Livourne 16
1050 Brussels
BELGIUM

Invoice no.   : 4593
Date   : 4 September 199–
Customer no. : 33202

Item:	No:	Units:	Price:	Total:
Jeans	4065-72	30	£69	£2,070
				£2,070

Payment within 30 days

We ordered 10 of each, small, medium and large. They sent all small

File 11

You are Pat Barton.

You have now been in Sydney for one week and your business partner, Chris James, is coming to join you. You have a free weekend before you start a busy round of meetings on Monday.

Tell your partner about some of the things you have done and seen and make suggestions for the weekend.

File 31

Look at this chart showing sales of soft drinks in the Americas and answer your partner's questions.

Results for Americas:

Country	Results	Reason
Canada	↓	competition
Mexico	↑	launch of new lemonade
Latin America	↑	new refillable packaging
Brazil	↓	recession
Argentina	↑	new distributor

Find out about sales of soft drinks in the Pacific Rim. You can ask questions like this:

Why did sales in New Zealand decrease?

Country	Results	Reason
New Zealand	↓	
Japan	↓	
Indonesia	↑	
Taiwan	↑	
Korea	↑	

File 27

Sell this product to your partner.

Use these phrases to help you.

This is our new …   *It's ideal for …*
It's made of …   *Another advantage is …*

File 19

You are Mr/Ms Le Blanc.

This is your diary for next week. You want to see Mr/Ms Schwarz on Thursday to discuss a new software program. Phone him/her to arrange a time.

Mon June 6

Tue June 7
SALES TRAINING

Wed June 8

Thu June 9

Fri June 10

Sat June 11

Sun June 12

When you have finished, write the appointment in your diary.
Then turn to File 21 on page 118.

File 9

Use your own name!

You are a colleague of Deborah Sauer. She's at lunch at the moment, so answer the phone and take any messages for her.

File 6

Use your own name!

You work in the Sales Department of ABC Computing. It is your job to deal with customer enquiries. Answer the phone and note the caller's name and address and what information s/he wants.

File 25

Use your own name!

You are going on a business trip.

Phone First Direct to find out the following exchange rates against pounds sterling:

- Hong Kong Dollars
- Japanese Yen
- Thai Baht
- Malaysian Ringgits.

File 35

You are a builder and are looking for a supplier of windows for some offices you are building. This is what you want. When you have finished, fill in what you get.

	You want	You get
Delivery	In two weeks	
Warranty	2 years	
Price	$5,000	
Discount	10%	
Credit period	60 days	

File 1

Your colleague has just sent you this fax, but the copy is very poor. Prepare questions to complete any missing information and check the details you have are correct. You can start like this:

Hello. This is (your name). I'm calling about a form from Sharon Willis. Can I just check the details with you?

SAVE 20% ON THE NEWSSTAND PRICE
You pay only £1.92 per issue instead of £2.40

Please write in BLOCK CAPITALS
Name Sharon Willis
Job title Software ...
Company name Lexus Ind ...

Address Brooklands,
Shropsh ...
Country UK
Tel. (01952) 677 166
Fax (01952) 677 159

I wish to pay by:
☐ Cheque
☒ Credit card
   ☐ Mastercard
   ☐ American Express
☒ Visa
Account number

Valid until 03.99
Signature

Your partner will ask you about the following subscription form.

SAVE 20% ON THE NEWSSTAND PRICE
You pay only £1.92 per issue instead of £2.40

Please write in BLOCK CAPITALS
Name Paul Harris
Job title Sales Manager
Company name
   Almera Enterprises
Address Hortonwood 21,
Weybridge, Surrey
Country UK
Tel. (01932) 816 003
Fax (01932) 816 395

I wish to pay by:
☐ Cheque
☒ Credit card
   ☐ Mastercard
   ☒ American Express
   ☐ Visa
Account number

Valid until 07.99
Signature

File 41

Women's share of jobs, European Union*, 1980s

Personal, catering and security services
Clerical
Sales workers and managers
Professional and technical
Agricultural
Government administration and managerial
Production, transport and construction

* Excluding Italy

0 10 20 30 40 50 60 70 80%

© *The Economist* 5th March 1994

File 7

Use your own name!

You are a colleague of Paul Taylor's. He's in a meeting at the moment, so answer the phone and take any messages for him.

When you have finished, turn to File 10 on page 120.

File 17

Use your own name!

You are Mr King's Personal Assistant at Omega Electronics. Mr McQueen is coming to visit your company next Friday. Phone his assistant and give him/her details of what you have planned.

Mr McQueen's Trip to Omega Electronics	
10.00	Meet Production Manager
11.30	Meet Sales Manager
13.00	Lunch at Little Chef Restaurant with Sales Manager
15.00	Tour of factory

Find out how Mr McQueen is planning to get to your company. If he is coming by train, offer to send a car to the station to meet him.

You can start like this:

This is ... . I'm calling to discuss Mr McQueen's visit next week.

File 13

Read the fact sheet about Sydney, Australia. From the information rate the facilities.

FACT SHEET **SYDNEY**	Rating – excellent ★★★
	satisfactory ★★
	poor ★

Transport facilities:

Air
Sydney has an international airport which services a large amount of passenger and cargo air traffic. The airport is running at full capacity and the need for a new airport is obvious. Delays and problems with air cargo are common. Strikes by ground crew are also a problem.

Rating .....

Rail
The railway network is quite extensive. However, there are some minor problems with cargo handling facilities.

Rating .....

Road
The highway system in Sydney is adequate for the transport of goods by road. Constant expansion of the highway and freeway system should result in Sydney having the road network necessary to meet future needs.

Rating .....

Port
Sydney has one of the finest natural harbours in the world. However, the cargo handling facilities are in need of upgrading so that they can load and unload ships faster.

Rating .....

Your partner has information on Singapore. Find out the good and bad features of the transport facilities in Singapore and make notes in the box.

Singapore	Rating
Air	
Rail	
Road	
Sea	

File 21

You are Mr/Ms Le Blanc.

You will receive a call from Mr/Ms Schwarz. Write any appointments you make in your diary on page 117.

File 29

This graph shows sales of the Airbus, 1990–1996. Use the information on the graph to complete the text. Then read it to your partner so they can draw the line on their graph.

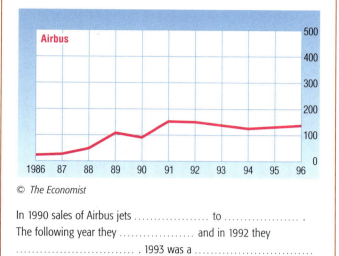

© *The Economist*

In 1990 sales of Airbus jets .... to ....

The following year they .... and in 1992 they

.... 1993 was a ....

year. Sales .... After that they

.... and in 1995 they ....

Finally they .... in 1996.

File 37

You are responsible for Credit Control at Cotton House.

Today's date is 7 October. Phone Josep Albiac and explain that you are still waiting for payment of this invoice.

COTTON HOUSE
HOO FARM ESTATE, KIDDERMINSTER, WORCESTERSHIRE

Josep Maria Albiac
C/Muntaner, 87
08036 Barcelona
SPAIN

Invoice no.   : 2643
Date   : 28 April 199–
Customer no. : 63101

Item:	No:	Units:	Price:	Total:
Jacket	9606-52	20	£159	£3,810
Shirt	8753-02	20	£99	£1,980
Waistcoat	8513-82	20	£79	£1,850
				£7,640

Payment within 30 days

When you have finished, turn to File 39 on page 116.

File 33

You work in the Personnel Department at Ahead Corporation.

Your boss has asked you to give a short presentation about the staff's needs for computer training.

This chart shows the number of people who attended courses last year, the number of people attending courses now and the number of people who will need courses in the future. Use it to help prepare your talk.

	Last year	Now	Next year
Basic computer training	20	60	8
Word processing	128	128	40
Spreadsheets	32	80	60
Database	16	32	32
Presentation	48	40	40

Listen to your partner talk about the company's needs for language training. Mark the things they do.

Say what they're going to talk about.

Introduce a topic.

Change the topic.

Conclude.

File 23

Use your own name!

You are going on a business trip to the USA. Phone First Direct to order US$500 in travellers' cheques. You need them in 10 days' time.

When you have finished, turn to File 26 on page 121.

File 44

MARKETING

Your task is to find ways of cutting marketing costs. This is the situation at present:

- Clients are often taken out to meals, invited to sports events, etc.
- Clients receive promotional gifts at New Year.

File 10

You are Leslie Aird from Celcius.

Phone Deborah Sauer at Gizmo Gadgets and tell her your flight gets in Friday at 9.30. Your flight number is BA 007.

File 43

Read this summary of a conversation. Then write what you think the people said like this:

> LAURA: *I think we should introduce a refill system.*

Laura suggested introducing a refill system for haircare products. Max agreed, but pointed out that it could be difficult to set up. James suggested putting a deposit on bottles to encourage people to return them to the store. Laura disagreed because refills would be cheaper as people didn't have to pay for the bottle.
Max suggested doing some market research and asked Laura to set it up.

When you have finished, compare with Learner A.

File 2

Your colleague has just sent you this fax, but the copy is very poor. Prepare questions to complete any missing information and check the details you have are correct. You can start like this:

Hello. This is (your name). I'm calling about a form from Paul Harris. Can I just check the details with you?

SAVE 20% ON THE NEWSSTAND PRICE
You pay only £1.92 per issue instead of £2.40

Please write in BLOCK CAPITALS	I wish to pay by:
Name Paul Harris	☐ Cheque
Job title Sales Manager	☒ Credit card
Company name	☐ Mastercard
A ...	☒ American Express
Address Hort ...	☐ Visa
Weybr ...	Account number
Country UK	
Tel. (01932) 816 003	Valid until 07.99
Fax (01932) 816 395	Signature

Your partner will ask you about the following subscription form.

SAVE 20% ON THE NEWSSTAND PRICE
You pay only £1.92 per issue instead of £2.40

Please write in BLOCK CAPITALS	I wish to pay by:
Name Sharon Willis	☐ Cheque
Job title Software engineer	☒ Credit card
Company name Lexus Industries	☐ Mastercard
	☐ American Express
Address Brooklands, Telford	☒ Visa
Shropshire	Account number
Country UK	
Tel. (01952) 677 166	Valid until 03.99
Fax (01952) 677 159	Signature

File 28

Sell this product to your partner.

Use these phrases to help you.

> *This is our new ...*   *It's ideal for ...*
> *It's made of ...*   *Another advantage is ...*

File 4

Use your own name!

You work in the Sales Department of ABC Computing. It is your job to deal with customer enquiries. Answer the phone and note the caller's name and address and what information s/he wants.

When you have finished, turn to File 5 on page 122.

File 20

You are Mr/Ms Schwarz.

You work for a company which develops computer software. You will receive a call from Mr/Ms Le Blanc. Write any arrangements you make in your diary.

Mon June 6	
Tue June 7	
Wed June 8	
Thu June 9	
Fri June 10	DAY OFF
Sat June 11	
Sun June 12	

When you have finished, write the appointment in your diary. Then turn to File 22 on page 123.

File 12

You are Chris James.

You've just arrived in Sydney to join your business partner, Pat Barton, who has already been there a week. You have a free weekend before you start a busy round of meetings on Monday. You want to see things, but you also need to recover from the flight and relax a little.

File 32

Look at this chart showing sales of soft drinks in the Pacific Rim and answer your partner's questions.

Results for Pacific Rim:

Country	Results	Reason
New Zealand	↓	competition + wet summer weather
Japan	↓	price increase
Indonesia	↑	new factory
Taiwan	↑	new distributor
Korea	↑	successful marketing campaign

Find out about the sales of soft drinks in the Americas. You can ask questions like this:

Why did sales in Canada decrease?

Country	Results	Reason
Canada	↓	
Mexico	↑	
Latin America	↑	
Brazil	↓	
Argentina	↑	

File 48

Use your own name!

Phone Le Montreux Palace hotel to find out about their conference facilities.

You need information on the following:

Meeting room for 40 people?
Lunch available? What?
Drinks available for breaks? What?
Prices?

File 36

You are a supplier of windows. This is what you want. When you have finished, fill in what you get.

	You want	You get
Delivery	In six weeks	
Warranty	6 months	
Price	$10,000	
Discount	0%	
Credit period	30 days	

File 15

Think about how you can describe this chart.

What questions will you ask your partner about their diagram?

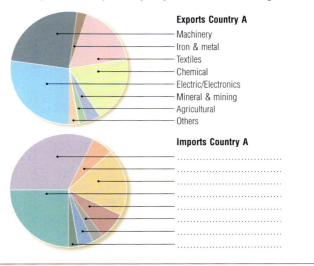

Exports Country A
- Machinery
- Iron & metal
- Textiles
- Chemical
- Electric/Electronics
- Mineral & mining
- Agricultural
- Others

Imports Country A

....
....
....
....
....
....
....
....
....

File 26

You work for First Direct. Remember to be friendly and efficient.

You can answer the phone like this:

Good morning. How can I help you?

and finish like this:

Is there anything else I can help you with?

Country	Currency	£1
Japan	Yen	160
Hong Kong	Dollar	11.40
Malaysia	Ringgit	3.73
Thailand	Baht	35.40

File 5

This is your business card.

KLA SYSTEMS

John/Joan Martin

PO Box 33
Coral Gables
FL 33124

You want some information about the *Vari-X* line. Phone ABC Computing and ask them to send you a brochure.

File 18

Use your own name!

You are Mr McQueen's assistant. You will receive a call from Mr King's assistant about his visit to Omega Electronics next week. Make notes on the itinerary and make sure he is seeing these people:

Production Manager
Sales Manager
Training Manager

Don't forget to tell them that Mr McQueen does not eat meat!

File 42

Read this conversation about introducing a refill system for Evergreen's haircare products. Then write a report like this:

Laura suggested introducing a refill system for the haircare products.

LAURA:	I think we should introduce a refill system for our haircare products.
MAX:	That's a good idea. But it might be difficult to set up.
JAMES:	Well, why don't we put a deposit on the bottles? That would encourage people to bring them back for a refill.
LAURA:	I don't think that's necessary. Refills would be cheaper anyway because people don't have to pay for the bottle.
MAX:	I think we should do some market research before we decide anything. Could you organize something, Laura?
LAURA:	Sure.

When you have finished, compare with Learner B.

File 45

SALES

Your task is to find ways of cutting costs in the sales department. This is the situation at present:

- Sales representatives stay in top hotels.
- Sales representatives usually travel first class.

File 14

Read the fact sheet about Singapore. From the information rate the facilities.

FACT SHEET **SINGAPORE**

Rating – excellent ***
satisfactory **
poor *

Transport facilities:

Air
Changi Airport in Singapore is one of the most modern airports in the world. It handles a huge number of passengers and a vast amount of freight each year and is the main air hub of Asia.

Rating .....

Rail
The railway network is limited. However, the facilities are adequate to satisfy the rail transportation needs of business.

Rating .....

Road
The road system in Singapore is adequate for the transport of goods by road. As road transport is not a major requirement of business this has not been given the same emphasis as air and sea facilities.

Rating .....

Port
Singapore has one of the busiest ports in the world with up-to-date cargo handling facilities and an efficient workforce. The government of Singapore realizes that Singapore's location on one of the world's most used seaways can be of great advantage if the facilities in port are first class, and they are.

Rating .....

Your partner has information on Sydney. Find out the good and bad features of the transport facilities in Sydney and write the main points in the box.

Sydney	Rating
Air	
Rail	
Road	
Sea	

File 30

This graph shows sales of the Boeing, 1986–1996. Use the information on the graph to complete the text. Then read it to your partner so they can draw the line on their graph.

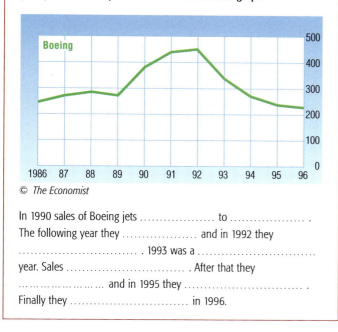

© The Economist

In 1990 sales of Boeing jets .... to ....
The following year they .... and in 1992 they
.... 1993 was a .... year. Sales .... After that they
.... and in 1995 they ....
Finally they .... in 1996.

File 40

You are responsible for Credit Control at Cotton House.

Today's date is 7 October. Phone Pierre Lecerf and explain that you are still waiting for payment of this invoice.

COTTON HOUSE
HOO FARM ESTATE, KIDDERMINSTER, WORCESTERSHIRE

Pierre Lecerf
Rue de Livourne 16
1050 Brussels
BELGIUM

Invoice no.   : 4593
Date   : 4 September 199–
Customer no. : 33202

Item:	No:	Units:	Price:	Total:
Jeans	4065-72	30	£69	£2,070
				£2,070

Payment within 30 days

File 34

You work in the Personnel Department at LinguaCom.

Your boss has asked you to give a short presentation about the staff's needs for language training.

This chart shows the number of people who attended courses last year, the number of people attending courses now and the number of people who will need courses in the future. Use it to help prepare your talk.

	Last year	Now	Next year
English	64	128	136
French	8	24	24
Spanish	0	32	40
German	0	16	16
Other	0	4	4

Listen to your partner talk about needs for computer training. Mark the things they do.

Say what they're going to talk about.	
Introduce a topic.	
Change the topic.	
Conclude.	

File 22

You are Mr/Ms Schwarz.

You have to go to Head Office on Thursday for an important meeting. Phone Mr/Ms Le Blanc and rearrange the appointment you made with him/her. (Use your diary from File 20 to help you.)

File 8

You are Michael/Michelle Wiltshire.

Phone Paul Taylor and ask him to bring the GMP file to the meeting on Thursday.

When you have finished, turn to File 9 on page 117.

File 38

You are Josep Maria Albiac.

Today's date is 7 October. You will get a phone call about this invoice.

COTTON HOUSE
Hoo Farm Estate, Kidderminster, Worcestershire

Josep Maria Albiac
C/Muntaner, 87
08036 Barcelona
SPAIN

Invoice no.   : 2643
Date   : 28 April 199–
Customer no. : 63101

Item:	No:	Units:	Price:	Total:
Jacket	9606-52	20	£159	£3,810
Shirt	8753-02	20	£99	£1,980
Waistcoat	8513-82	20	£79	£1,850
				£7,640

Payment within 30 days

£159 x 20 = £3180
£79 x 20 = £1580
Total = £6740

When you have finished, turn to File 40 on page 123.

File 49

Use your own name!

You work for Le Montreux Palace hotel.

You will receive a phone call from someone enquiring about the hotel's conference facilities. Use this information to answer their questions.

Daily Conference Package

Air-conditioned conference room.

Two coffee breaks with coffee, tea, juice and mineral water.

3-course business lunch.

Flipchart, pads and pens.

All technical equipment available upon request.

Daily delegate rate CHF 85.–

LE MONTREUX PALACE

File 24

You work for First Direct. Remember to be friendly and efficient.

You can answer the phone like this:

Good morning. How can I help you?

and finish like this:

Is there anything else I can help you with?

When you have finished, turn to File 25 on page 117.

File 46

OVERHEADS

Your task is to find ways of cutting overheads. This is the situation at present:

- Cleaners come in 7–9 p.m. every day.
- Offices are heated to 20°C all year round.

File 16

Think about how you can describe this chart.

What questions will you ask your partner about their diagram?

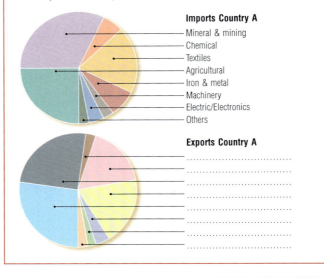

Imports Country A
- Mineral & mining
- Chemical
- Textiles
- Agricultural
- Iron & metal
- Machinery
- Electric/Electronics
- Others

Exports Country A
....
....
....
....
....
....
....
....

File 3

This is your business card.

ZIRCON INSTRUMENTS

Paul/Paula Tullet

4000 Fitch Street
Mobile AL 33640

You want some information about the *Vu-Tec* range of filters. Phone ABC Computing and ask them to send you a brochure.
When you have finished turn to File 6 on page 117.

Tapescripts

1.1 B

Conversation one

WOMAN 1:	Hello. I don't think we've met. My name's Gina Lee.
MAN 1:	And I'm Paulo Mendes. Pleased to meet you, Ms Lee.
WOMAN 1:	Where are you from, Mr Mendes?
MAN 1:	Brazil, Rio de Janeiro, to be exact. I work for Ark. Perhaps you've heard of them? I'm a software engineer there. And what about you? What do you do?
WOMAN 1:	I'm in hardware development with Cor.
MAN 1:	That's interesting. Perhaps you can tell me something about …

Conversation two

WOMAN 2:	Wendy, do you know Dirk Dressler? Dirk, this is Wendy James from United Finance.
MAN 2:	I don't think we've met before. Nice to meet you, Ms James.
WOMAN 3:	How do you do? Please call me Wendy.
MAN 2:	And I'm Dirk.
WOMAN 3:	What exactly do you do, Dirk?
MAN 2:	I'm responsible for quality control. I …

Conversation three

MAN 3:	Hello Mikiko. Nice to see you again.
WOMAN 4:	Hi Oscar. How are you?
MAN 3:	Fine thanks. And you?
WOMAN 4:	Oh, not too bad. How are things in Sydney?
MAN 3:	Pretty good. We're quite busy at the moment. But I'll tell you about that later. Did you have a good flight?
WOMAN 4:	Well, we were late taking off, but …

1.2 B

MAN:	Are you Ms Novak?
WOMAN:	Yes, that's right.
MAN:	I'm Bruno Soares, the Sales Manager. How do you do?
WOMAN:	How do you do? It's nice to finally meet you – to put a face to a name.
MAN:	Yes, it is, isn't it? Now, come this way and we'll go up to my office. Is this your first trip to Porto?
WOMAN:	Yes, it is. I've been to Lisbon a couple of times before, but this is the first time I've been to Porto.
MAN:	And what do you think of it?
WOMAN:	It seems like a nice place. Do you live in Porto itself?
MAN:	No, I don't. I live to the north. It's about twenty minutes from here, depending on the traffic. And what about yourself? Which part of the States are you from?
WOMAN:	The Midwest. From Omaha, Nebraska. Have you ever been there?
MAN:	No, I haven't, unfortunately. How long are you staying in Porto?
WOMAN:	Until Friday. And then I'm heading north. To Belgium.
MAN:	Right, here we are. Now can I get you a drink before we start …

1.3 B

THOMAS:	Pamela Thomas. Good morning.
CHANG:	Good morning. This is Brenda Chang from Asia Business Publications. I'm calling about your subscription for *The Economist*.
THOMAS:	Oh yes.
CHANG:	I'm afraid your fax isn't very clear, so I'd just like to check some of the details.
THOMAS:	Of course.
CHANG:	Right. Your first name's Pamela, isn't it?
THOMAS:	That's right.
CHANG:	And you work for Extratour, don't you?
THOMAS:	Yes.
CHANG:	Now, I'm afraid I can't read your job title at all. What do you do, Ms Thomas?
THOMAS:	I'm an accountant.
CHANG:	Right. And I can't read the name of the street either.
THOMAS:	That's Bourke Street. That's B-O-U-R-K-E.
CHANG:	And that's in Melbourne, isn't it?
THOMAS:	Yes, that's right.
CHANG:	OK. Now, you want to pay by Mastercard, don't you?
THOMAS:	Yes.
CHANG:	Could you give me your account number?
THOMAS:	Sure. It's 5412 0012 4567.
CHANG:	Right then, I think that's everything. You should get your first copy in a couple of weeks.
THOMAS:	Thanks very much.

2.1 D

INTERVIEWER:	What's the name of your company?
EMPLOYEE:	The Atlas Copco Group.
INTERVIEWER:	What line of business are you in?
EMPLOYEE:	We're in the mining and industrial sectors.
INTERVIEWER:	What goods or services does your company provide?
EMPLOYEE:	We make compressors and other equipment for the mining and construction industries.
INTERVIEWER:	How many employees does your company have?
EMPLOYEE:	Over 21,000 world-wide.
INTERVIEWER:	Where are your headquarters?
EMPLOYEE:	In Sweden, in the capital, Stockholm.
INTERVIEWER:	Where are your main markets?
EMPLOYEE:	Well, we operate world-wide, but our main market is the European Union.

2.3 C

Call one

TONG:	ABC Computing. Good morning.
REINER:	Oh, good morning. This is Paul Reiner from AFC. I'm interested in your *Vu-Tec* filters.
TONG:	I'll send you our brochure. Could I have your name and address?
REINER:	Sure. My name's Paul Reiner. That's R-E-I-N-E-R.
TONG:	R-E-I-N-E-R.
REINER:	And my address is AFC, 524 West Capitol Street in Little Rock, Arkansas.
TONG:	Right. And the zip code?
REINER:	72601.

TONG:	72601. OK. I'll mail you a brochure today, Mr Reiner.
REINER:	Thanks very much.
TONG:	You're welcome.

Call two

TONG:	ABC Computing. Good morning.
ANDERSEN:	Could you send me some information about your *Vari-X* filters?
TONG:	I'll send you our brochure. Could I have your name and address?
ANDERSEN:	Sure. My name's Erica Andersen. That's A-N-D-E-R-S-E-N.
TONG:	A-N-D-E-R-S-E-N.
ANDERSEN:	And my address is TAZ Technologies. 24 Otis Street.
TONG:	Sorry. Could you please spell the name of the street for me?
ANDERSEN:	Otis. That's O-T-I-S. San Francisco. California 94103.
TONG:	94103. OK. I'll put a brochure and price lists in the mail today, Ms Andersen.
ANDERSEN:	Thanks very much.
TONG:	You're welcome.

3.1 B

Now today I'll start off by telling you a little about the structure of Comex Xpress. The head of the company here in Glasgow is the CEO or Chief Executive Office, and that's Mr Bateman.

Now, as you know, Comex Xpress is divided into four divisions: Production, Finance, Sales and Human Resources. The first division here is production and that is headed by the Plant Manager, Tom McEwan. The Technicians, Maintenance Officers and Quality Controllers all report to him, as do the Packaging and Dispatch Clerks.

The next division is Finance and this department is headed by the Chief Accountant – Joshua Goldfinger. The Accounts Clerks and Credit Controllers, who check that customers have settled their invoices, report to him as does the Purchasing Officer.

Then we come onto the Marketing division which is both sales and marketing. The head of Marketing is Ms Julie Nicolson. She's responsible for the Export Clerks, the Sales Representatives who are on the road, and After-sales Clerks who deal with any problems that arise with our products.

Finally we have the Human Resources department, headed by Sheila Barrett. You met the Recruitment Officer Fiona Lewis at your interviews. Then there's myself, the Training Officer and finally the Pay Clerk – Ian Weir – so if you have any queries about salaries and so on you should go and see him …

3.2 B

Interview one

INTERVIEWER:	What do you do, Frank?
FRANK:	I work in Accounts, I'm responsible for invoicing our customers.
INTERVIEWER:	And what are you doing at the moment?
FRANK:	I'm sending out reminders to all our customers who haven't settled last year's invoices yet.

Interview two

INTERVIEWER:	Tell me something about your work, Suzanne.
SUZANNE:	I work in Human Resources. I'm in charge of training, er that's both for new employees such as school leavers and for employees who have already been here a while. I find trainers, organize venues, things like that.
INTERVIEWER:	And what are you doing at the moment?
SUZANNE:	Right now I'm planning the training programme for next year.

Interview three

INTERVIEWER:	What do you do, Peter?
PETER:	I work in Technical Services. We deal with customer problems, er, provide customers with spare parts, repair machines that break down, that kind of thing.
INTERVIEWER:	And what are you doing at the moment?
PETER:	Well, the company has just launched a new machine, so I'm actually preparing for a trade fair.

Interview four

INTERVIEWER:	What do you do, Uschi?
USCHI:	I work in Marketing. I answer customers' questions about our products. I also travel a lot, I give product presentations to our customers.
INTERVIEWER:	And what are you doing at the moment?
USCHI:	I'm running a training course for the new sales reps.

Interview five

INTERVIEWER:	Tell me something about your work, Rolando.
ROLANDO:	I work in the Purchasing Department. I'm responsible for buying everything the company needs – from ball-point pens through to the raw materials and components we need to make our products.
INTERVIEWER:	And what are you doing at the moment?
ROLANDO:	Well, people in Accounts have asked for some new chairs, so I'm looking for a supplier of office furniture.

Interview six

INTERVIEWER:	What do you do, Elke?
ELKE:	I work in EDP. I'm in charge of software development and maintenance. I also run a hotline for our employees if they have problems with their computers or programs.
INTERVIEWER:	And what are you doing at the moment?
ELKE:	I'm testing some new software for our sales force.

3.3 A

Call one

RECEPTION:	Gizmo Gadgets. Good morning.
CALLER 1:	Oh, good morning. This is Hugh Payne from Head Office speaking. Could you put me through to Stephanie Crooke in Accounts, please?
RECEPTION:	Hold the line, please … I'm afraid the line's engaged. Would you like to leave a message?
CALLER 1:	Er, yes, please. Could you ask her to send the list of last month's payments to head office by Friday the fourteenth at the latest?
RECEPTION:	Last month's figures to head office by Friday, the fourteenth. Who's calling, please?
CALLER 1:	Hugh Payne. That's P-A-Y-N-E.
RECEPTION:	Right, Mr Payne, I'll give Ms Crooke the message.
CALLER 1:	Thanks very much.
RECEPTION:	You're welcome.

Call two

RECEPTION:	Gizmo Gadgets. Good morning.
CALLER 2:	Hello. This is Tanya Cordrey from EKS. I'd like to speak to Stephen Stern in Sales.
RECEPTION:	Hold the line, please. … I'm afraid he's in a meeting until 12. Can I take a message?
CALLER 2:	Oh, yes. Mm. Could you ask him to call me about my order, that's order number 3754, either sometime today or tomorrow before nine?
RECEPTION:	Order number 3754, today, or tomorrow before nine. Who's speaking please?

CALLER 2: Tanya Cordrey from –
RECEPTION: Sorry, could you spell that please?
CALLER 2: Sure. That's C-O-R-D-R-E-Y.
RECEPTION: C-O-R-D-R-E-Y. And your telephone number?
CALLER 2: 293 544.
RECEPTION: Right, Ms Cordrey. I'll give him the message.
CALLER 2: Thank you.
RECEPTION: You're welcome.

3.3 B

RECEPTION: Gizmo Gadgets. Good morning.
CALLER: Hello. This is Rosie Grunwald from Bit and Byte. I'd like to speak to Mr Brunner.
RECEPTION: Hold the line, please. … Hello. I'm afraid there's no reply. Would you like to leave your name and number, and I'll get him to call you back.
CALLER: Oh, thank you. My name's Rosie Grunwald. That's G-R-U-N-W-A-L-D. Could you ask him to call me back about the computer workshop for the marketing department? My number's 665 433 and –
RECEPTION: Sorry, what was the number?
CALLER: 665 433.
RECEPTION: I'll just repeat that. Call Rosie Grunwald on 665 433 about the computer workshop for the marketing department.
CALLER: That's it. Thanks a lot.
RECEPTION: You're welcome.

4.1 B

Conversation one
CAREY: Would you like to have dinner with me tonight?
HAWLEY: That's very nice of you, but I'm afraid I'm still a little jet lagged from my trip and I'd like to make it an early night.
CAREY: Perhaps some time later in the week?
HAWLEY: Yes, that would be nice. Thank you.

Conversation two
CAREY: We're having a barbecue at my place on Wednesday. Would you like to come?
HAWLEY: Yes, that sounds great. I'd love to. What time?
CAREY: Around seven o'clock. Er, would you like me to arrange for someone to pick you up from your hotel?
HAWLEY: That's very nice of you. Thanks a lot.

Conversation three
CAREY: Do you have any plans for the weekend?
HAWLEY: Well, I thought I might do a little sightseeing, I haven't had time to see much of Sydney yet.
CAREY: Well, how about a harbour cruise on Saturday? You get a fantastic view of the city.
HAWLEY: That would be great. I'd love that.
CAREY: Good. I'll get some tickets.

4.2 C

WOMAN: Well, I think the meeting went well today.
MAN: Yes, it did. But it's good to have a break from business.
WOMAN: So what do you do when you're not working?
MAN: Well, as I sit at a desk most of the day, I like to try and keep fit. I do quite a lot of sport.
WOMAN: Oh, yes. What do you do?
MAN: I enjoy cycling. Mountain biking actually.
WOMAN: I suppose it's a good place to do it here.
MAN: Yes, it is. And I've just taken up sailing.
WOMAN: Really? I didn't know there was any water around here.
MAN: Well, there's a couple of lakes nearby. But I prefer to go away – weekend breaks. What about yourself? Do you do any sports?
WOMAN: Well, I try and go jogging a couple of times a week. But I'm not really interested in sports. I love gardening. Otherwise I prefer to relax. I love going to the cinema. And I'm a real bookworm.
MAN: Really. What kind of things do you like reading?
WOMAN: Well, there's nothing that beats a really good murder!
MAN: You don't look the type for that!
WOMAN: Oh, you'd be surprised …

4.3 C

INTERVIEWER: Excuse me. I'm doing some market research. Can I ask you a few questions?
WOMAN: Yes, of course. Go ahead.
INTERVIEWER: Right. Do you travel for business?
WOMAN: Yes, I do. On average I'd say I spend two or three days a week visiting customers.
INTERVIEWER: Right … 'regularly'. Now, do you ever work at home?
WOMAN: No, I don't. I'm so seldom at home, I don't want to have to work there too!
INTERVIEWER: OK. Next question. Do you ever make presentations?
WOMAN: Yes, I do.
INTERVIEWER: How often do you do that?
WOMAN: Let me see. Two or three times a month maybe. Some months it's more, some months it's less.
INTERVIEWER: Right. Let's say … 'often'. Now, do you usually do your own typing?
WOMAN: I'm afraid so. I don't have anyone to do it for me.
INTERVIEWER: OK. And do you use a computer at work?
WOMAN: Sure. I'd be lost without it!
INTERVIEWER: OK, I'll mark that 'regularly'. Do you ever buy computer magazines?
WOMAN: No, I don't. Never.
INTERVIEWER: Right. And one last question … could you just look at this and tell me which age bracket you're in …

5

INTERVIEWER: Christine, you're not only a typical eighteen year old, studying for your A levels; you're also a very successful businesswoman. How do you manage to combine these two things? Perhaps you could tell me about a typical day?
CHRISTINE: Sure. Well, I usually get up about five o'clock. I try to get to the office for seven and then design jewellery for an hour and a half until it's time to dash off to school which starts at a quarter to nine.
INTERVIEWER: And then you're at school all day?
CHRISTINE: No, not at all. When the others go off for lunch, I go back to the office for another hour's work.
INTERVIEWER: What time do you finish school?
CHRISTINE: Half past three.
INTERVIEWER: What do you do then?
CHRISTINE: It's back to the office until about nine. This is when people who manufacture jewellery for me bring it in for distribution – I also have to give them new supplies – it's quite chaotic!
INTERVIEWER: So when do you find time to study?
CHRISTINE: After that. I usually do about three hours' revision before I go to bed at midnight.
INTERVIEWER: What are you going to do when you finish school?

CHRISTINE: I plan to do business studies at Birmingham University.
INTERVIEWER: Do you really need to? I mean, you already have a lot of business experience.
CHRISTINE: Er, I expect it'll be a little strange to learn the theory after having been involved in the practical side since I was thirteen. But –
INTERVIEWER: What do your school friends think of this?
CHRISTINE: They've always thought I was a little different. They were interested in music, I was interested in business and politics.
INTERVIEWER: Do you have time for a social life?
CHRISTINE: As I make and sell jewellery, when I do go out, I'm more interested in what people are wearing than enjoying myself. I never turn off!

6.2 A

INTERVIEWER: How do you recommend that your clients send their goods overseas?
MAN: Well, there's no simple answer to that, it depends on a number of factors. For example, if speed is essential, we recommend air freight. It's faster than any other means of transportation.
INTERVIEWER: But that's very expensive, isn't it?
MAN: Sure. But it's better to pay more than to be late delivering the goods. And in one way it isn't expensive at all. Insurance for air freight is cheap, much cheaper than for sea freight.
INTERVIEWER: So do you ever recommend shipping goods sea freight?
MAN: Oh, yes. If a client has large quantities or very heavy machinery, it's the only answer. But it's much slower. And port fees and delays can make it just as expensive as air freight.
INTERVIEWER: What about goods that are transported nationally? Do you recommend truck or rail?
MAN: Well usually truck because you can deliver direct to the customer. Its advantage over rail is that it isn't dependent on a set route, so it's much more flexible. One problem with road transportation is the pollution factor and this is where rail has a definite advantage. Rail is also more economical in the use of labour. You can transport up to sixty carloads of goods with a small crew.

6.3 B

DAVISON: This is Brian Davison speaking. I'm afraid I'm not in my office at the moment, but if you would like to leave a message, I will return your call as soon as possible.
SANCHEZ: This is Manuela Sanchez from Royale Engineering in San Sebastian, Spain. I'm calling about the delivery conditions for our order for machine spare parts, er, that's order number A 5490, er, we arranged delivery by ship from Southampton to Bilbao, but I'm afraid that something has come up and we now need the consignment rather urgently. Would it be possible for you to send it air freight to San Sebastian as soon as possible? Of course, we will pay any additional costs that arise. Thank you very much.

7.1 B

MEXICAN: Our main export is petroleum and petroleum products. Many people don't know this, but Mexico has one of the largest oil reserves in the world outside the Middle East. And so it's a very important industry for our country. In fact, it's one of our main employers.
INTERVIEWER: What about hi-tech industries such as the computer industry?
MEXICAN: Well, although we still import most of our needs in this area, a number of American, Japanese and Taiwanese hi-tech companies are now producing their products in Mexico. We expect this sort of cooperation to continue and that Mexican companies will soon start producing their own hi-tech equipment to export to other countries.

In other manufacturing areas we are quite strong. We have a growing textile industry and a thriving automobile industry. Volkswagen, General Motors and Ford all have large plants here and we expect other foreign car manufacturers to relocate too.
INTERVIEWER: What about the pharmaceutical and chemical industries?
MEXICAN: We rely on imports to cover our needs in this area.
INTERVIEWER: And other industries?
MEXICAN: Well, agriculture is important. We produce a lot of fruit and vegetables for the local and North American market. And another developing industry is tourism. We have such beauty and diversity of countryside as well as history and culture that it is easy to understand why Mexico is one of the most popular tourist destinations in the world, and I'm very proud to be part of such an important industry …

8.1 B

OLIVIA: Let's just go over the arrangements for my trip to Bombay.
ASSISTANT: Sure, here's your schedule. You're flying at 9.55 on Monday evening. That's British Airways flight 139. Er, you have to check in two hours before so I've arranged for a car to pick you up from the office at 6.30.
OLIVIA: Good. What time does the flight get into Bombay?
ASSISTANT: It gets into Bombay at 11.15 p.m. That's local time, of course. Er, I've booked you a room at the Oberoi. They're sending a car to pick you up.
OLIVIA: Fine. Now when am I seeing Mr Shah?
ASSISTANT: Tuesday afternoon at two. By the way, Mr Majundar is coming to the meeting as well.
OLIVIA: That's good news, we won't have to arrange a separate meeting. And has the tour of the new plant in Bombay and the meeting with the directors been arranged for Wednesday?
ASSISTANT: Yes, they'll pick you up in the morning at 9, and plan to show you the plant, take you to lunch, and return you to the hotel at about 5 p.m.
OLIVIA: Good. Now, has my visa arrived?
ASSISTANT: No, not yet. I'll phone the embassy and find out if they've sent it off yet.
OLIVIA: Thanks. And could you order some travellers' cheques?
ASSISTANT: Sure, I'll phone the bank.
OLIVIA: And when am I flying back?
ASSISTANT: I'm afraid the earliest flight I could get is Thursday at 1.15 a.m., everything else was booked up. That's British Airways again, flight 138. That gets you back into London at 6.25 Thursday morning. You've got Thursday in London for the Sales Meeting, but not until 3 p.m., then Friday morning you're leaving for New York …

8.2 C

JEFF: I've just been on the phone to HQ. They're having problems with their new software so I'm going to have to go down to Orlando next week.

ASSISTANT: Do you want to stay at the Marriot?

JEFF: Yes. You'd better book me a room for three nights. From the 19th to the 21st.

ASSISTANT: Right. There's one slight problem. The meeting with Mr Wong at Orion is on the 21st. Should I cancel it?

JEFF: Yes. Maybe you can suggest a new date. Or no, tell him I'll get in touch with him when I get back …

8.3 A

Call one

IAN: Ian Norman speaking.

KATE: Hello Ian, this is Kate. How are you?

IAN: Fine, fine. And yourself?

KATE: A bit stressed with the new catalogue at the moment. It's got to be at the printers by the end of the month. Actually, that's the reason I'm ringing you. Can we fix a time to discuss it?

IAN: Sure. When would be convenient?

KATE: Well, are you free next Monday?

IAN: Yes, as far as I know. I'll just check my diary. Er, what time?

KATE: Early morning would suit me best. Shall we say ten o'clock? In my office?

IAN: Er, yes, that's fine.

KATE: Right. Then I'll see you on Monday at ten.

Call two

KATE: Kate Williams.

SECRETARY: Good morning. This is Brian Matthew's secretary. Mr Matthews will be in Bristol on Monday and he'd like to see you to discuss the marketing plan for next spring. Can we fix a time?

KATE: Sure. When would suit him best?

SECRETARY: Well, he's got quite a full schedule already. Would eleven o'clock be OK?

KATE: I'll just have a look. I've actually got a meeting then. But I can try and change it.

SECRETARY: That would be a great help.

KATE: I'll get back to you in a minute.

SECRETARY: Thanks very much.

8.3 C

IAN: This is Ian Norman speaking. Please leave a message after the signal.

KATE: Hello, Ian. This is Kate again. The reason I'm calling is that something's come up, I have to see Brian Matthews from Head Office at eleven on Monday. Could we meet a little earlier, say nine fifteen? Could you give me a ring to confirm it? Thanks very much.

9.1 C

FIRST DIRECT: Hello, this is First Direct, how can I help you?

MAN: This is Ahmed Aziz speaking. Er, I'm interested in opening an account with you, but I have a couple of questions.

FIRST DIRECT: What exactly would you like to know, Mr Aziz?

MAN: First of all, if I bank with you, how do I pay money into my account?

FIRST DIRECT: Well, as you probably know, First Direct is a part of the Midland Bank. That means you can pay into your First Direct account at any of their branches.

MAN: I see. Er, do they charge me for that?

FIRST DIRECT: No, that's free.

MAN: OK. Right. The other thing I wanted to know was do you pay interest on current accounts?

FIRST DIRECT: Yes, we do. As long as your account is in credit. The interest is then calculated daily, and we add it to your account at the end of each month.

MAN: Uh uh.

FIRST DIRECT: Is there anything else you'd like to know, Mr Aziz?

MAN: No, I think that's all for the time being. Thank you. Goodbye.

FIRST DIRECT: Thank you for calling, Mr Aziz. Goodbye.

9.2 B

SALES REP: Right. Now this range of children's furniture is ideal from toddlers all the way through to teenagers. As you know, a child's needs change quite quickly in the first few years of their life so you need something that is flexible. Here you can start off with one or two basic items and then add more as the child gets older, a wardrobe, more shelves, perhaps a desk once they start school.

Now let me start by showing you the bed. Would you like to come over here? Now this is a standard size single bed.

CUSTOMER: How long is it? We don't have a lot of space, so every centimetre counts.

SALES REP: Outside measurements are 204 centimetres by 101.5 centimetres.

CUSTOMER: Uh uh. That should fit. And how high is it? It looks quite high.

SALES REP: 172 cm. So you can have a play area underneath or, if necessary, add a second bed. It's made of solid wood and comes in a natural wood finish as you see it here. It's also available with turquoise and red applications.

CUSTOMER: It looks very nice. How much does it cost?

SALES REP: The basic bed as you see it here is $399.

CUSTOMER: I see. And what about delivery times?

SALES REP: About six weeks from date of order.

CUSTOMER: Do we have to pick it up?

SALES REP: No, no, we deliver anywhere within Metro Toronto, and …

9.3 A

First call

PRINTER: Phoenix Printers. Good morning.

AUSTIN: This is Jennifer Austin from Leroy Motors. Could I speak to Leo Dayton, please?

PRINTER: I'm afraid he's not in at the moment. Can I give him a message?

AUSTIN: Well, I'm ringing about a reprint of one of our brochures. I asked him to do it six weeks ago and we're still waiting for them. If I remember rightly, I did say it was rather urgent.

PRINTER: I'll get him to call you back as soon as he comes in, Ms Austin.

AUSTIN: Thank you very much.

Second call

AUSTIN: This is Jennifer Austin speaking.

DAYTON: Leo Dayton from Phoenix Printers. I understand there's been a problem with an order.

AUSTIN: That's right. I asked you to do a reprint of our A90 brochure some time ago and we still don't have it.

DAYTON:	Yes. I've just been trying to find out what happened. It seems some urgent work came in and your order got overlooked. I'm really sorry.
AUSTIN:	I see. Well, the problem is we have an exhibition coming up at the beginning of next month and we'll want to have them for then. How soon can you get them done?
DAYTON:	Would the end of the week be OK?
AUSTIN:	That would be great.
DAYTON:	Right, then. I'll see that you get them by Friday. And I'm really sorry about this.
AUSTIN:	Don't worry.

9.3 D

Message one
Hello. This is Anne Wallace. Er, we had a meeting yesterday afternoon at three. Did you forget? Please give me a call so we can arrange a new time. Thank you.

Message two
Hello. This is Max van der Valk from Gamma International in Holland. We've just accepted delivery of a consignment of A45 motors. Unfortunately, there were no operating instructions included. Could you send us them as soon as possible? Thanks.

Message three
Hello. This is Arturo Hernandez from Enigma Engineering. I'm still waiting for you to return my call about the problems we're having with the C60 motors. I thought you were going to ring last week. Please call me as soon as possible. I'll be in my office today until three.

10

INTERVIEWER:	Mr Shaw, you recently changed banks. Can you tell us something about that?
SHAW:	Certainly.
INTERVIEWER:	How long were you with your old bank?
SHAW:	Five years.
INTERVIEWER:	And why did you decide to change?
SHAW:	Well, I'm self-employed, er, I work as a financial adviser, and my income varies from month to month. So I need an overdraft facility to cope with this. At my old bank, the overdraft facility was limited and then, when I compared the charges with the rates of my new bank, I realized I was paying far too much. Er, I might have stayed with my old bank, but then a credit card was stolen. The manager who handled the incident was unpleasant and unsympathetic. I think he forgot that I was the customer. And so I decided to change.
INTERVIEWER:	Are you satisfied with your new bank?
SHAW:	So far, yes. I now pay less for my overdraft and so far, I've found my new bank very helpful. It's also very convenient for me because there is a branch close by and plenty of cash points.
INTERVIEWER:	So you don't regret the move?
SHAW:	No. And although it seems complicated at first, I'd certainly recommend switching banks if you're not happy with your present one.

11.1 B

INTERVIEWER:	The British Broadcasting Corporation recently changed its logo. Can you tell us why?
BBC:	Well, we were planning the launch of a range of new channels and services at the time, so it was an opportunity for us to think over the existing logo.

INTERVIEWER:	You weren't happy with it?
BBC:	Basically no. There were a number of problems. For example, it didn't work as an on-screen graphic. Because it sat at an angle, it often appeared to vibrate and the colours disappeared. Then, being four-colour, it was expensive to use. And finally, we felt the BBC had become visually fragmented over the years. By that I mean we had too many sub-logos which weakened the effect of the main brand. With the new logo, the 'BBC' is much stronger and emphasizes the brand.
INTERVIEWER:	So what were your main aims in changing the logo?
BBC:	They were twofold. First, to simplify the design of the logo. Second, to use it as a unifying symbol across all BBC departments and services.
INTERVIEWER:	And do you think the new logo has been a success?
BBC:	I'd say yes. As I said, we wanted something that was simple to use and this logo works well in all media. And I think the design manages to reflect our core values of quality, accuracy and artisic excellence in an increasingly international and competitive news market. So yes, I think it has been a success.
INTERVIEWER:	What about the costs?
BBC:	So far, it's cost us about £1.7 million. Now that may seem a lot of money, but in the long term it will actually save us money because, for example, we will save on print costs by not having to use four colours each time the logo is used.

11.3 A

Right. Now, about this new store we're opening. We've decided that on the day it opens, each customer who buys something in the store will receive a promotional gift. I think we can expect a good turnout on the first day. We'll be advertising in the local press the week beforehand and on billboards, and on local radio. We've allocated a budget of £2,500 for this promotional opening, and what I'd like you to do is to find a suitable gift. Or, er, gifts, I don't think it necessarily has to be the same for everyone. I think we can expect a lot of young mothers, and also a lot of teenagers and I think you should aim for about 5,000 items.

Now the one thing that is important is that the promotional items should have our name embossed on them. If you have any questions, I'll be back in the office at the beginning of next week.

12.2 B

Extract one
We've had an excellent year in the UK with an increase in both profits and sales over last year. I think we can safely say this result is due to our mid-year promotional push, in which we visited almost 7,000 customer outlets in two weeks and displayed over 210,000 cases of Fizzo.

Extract two
I'm afraid we've had a rather disappointing year in Continental Europe. Competition has been fierce and sales of Fizzo have declined. Er, this is not only a result of the recession we've been going through, but also of the fall in the number of tourists in the Mediterranean countries and poor summer weather. Despite all this, we have still managed to make a small profit.

Extract three
Fizzo has performed very well in North America and both sales and profits are up again. These results are due to our Total Quality Management programme which has led to significant improvements in product quality, customer service and productivity.

Extract four

In Australia sales have fallen because of the recession, competition and poor summer weather. Investment in new products means that profits have fallen too, but we expect next year's results to be better.

Extract five

Sales and profits in Africa were up this year. This was due to improved production facilities, along with launching Fizzo in new bottles.

12.3 B

Good afternoon, ladies and gentlemen. Welcome to Marea. My name's John Snow and I'm the training manager. I'm going to talk to you briefly about our new in-house training programme.

Let's start by looking backwards. As you know, the last few years have been a time of change at Marea. Although sales of our products have increased dramatically, so has the competition.

Last year we took a long hard look at the way we do things here and we talked to all our staff to try and identify areas for improvements. One of the results of this has been the installation of PCs at nearly all workplaces. A second one has been the need for staff training, and that is why we have now decided to set up our own in-house training programme.

Let's move on and have a look at this training programme …

13.1 B

CUSTOMER:	What kind of price did you have in mind?
SUPPLIER:	The list price is $24,999.
CUSTOMER:	That seems rather high for a good customer. Will you give me a discount if I pay cash?
SUPPLIER:	I should think we can come to some kind of agreement.
CUSTOMER:	Good. And what about delivery? When can you deliver the machine?
SUPPLIER:	Well, we've got rather a backlog of orders at the moment. I should think it'll take somewhere between four and five months.
CUSTOMER:	Hm. I was hoping for three.
SUPPLIER:	Well, that's rather difficult at the moment. But if you're prepared to wait, we'll give you a reduction in price …

13.2 B

PRESENTER:	Bad payers are making life miserable for many of Britain's small businesses. As the recession and high interest rates hit company finances, many businesses are trying to improve their own cash flow by not paying their suppliers. Here's a report from Simon Anderson, our Economics correspondent.
ANDERSON:	A new survey on overdue payments out this week shows that the majority of British companies are not paid within the standard 30-day credit period, but an average of 78 days later. Is this situation unique to Britain? Looking at the rest of Europe, the answer seems to be no. But it is only in France and Italy that the situation is worse. Italians take an average of 90 days to settle their accounts; the French a grand total of 108. However, it is only fair to add that in both France and Italy the agreed credit period is 60 days compared to our 30 days.
Travelling further north, people seem to be better at getting paid. Like us, the Scandinavians have an agreed credit period of 30 days; in both Sweden and Denmark, the average period of payment is 48 days and in Finland 55. There are several reasons for this. Firstly, there are …

13.3 B

CHEZDOY:	Redress, good morning.
PATEL:	This is Tara Patel from Cotton House in Kidderminster. Could I speak to Mr Chezdoy, please?
CHEZDOY:	Speaking.
PATEL:	Ah, hello, Mr Chezdoy. I'm calling about an outstanding invoice. Er, that's invoice number 523 705 from the 3rd April.
CHEZDOY:	Just a minute. I'll check our records. Sorry, what was the invoice number again?
PATEL:	523 705.
CHEZDOY:	Ah, here it is. 523 705, the 3rd April. Yes, I remember. That was an order for baseball caps and belts. Total amount £1,050. Er, there's a note attached saying we're still waiting for the rest of the delivery. We've only received the belts so far, the baseball caps haven't arrived yet.
PATEL:	Oh, I'm sorry. I didn't realize the order was incomplete. Our new software automatically prints outstanding payments at the beginning of the month.
CHEZDOY:	Don't worry. But I'll send you a cheque as soon as we receive the goods.
PATEL:	Good. Anyway, I'm sorry again, Mr Chezdoy. Thanks for your help. Goodbye.

14.1 C

INTERVIEWER:	It's always nice to receive a gift from a business partner, but what is acceptable? I mean, when does a gift stop being a gift and become a bribe?
KELLY:	Well, that depends largely on the company. In America, we've found that many large corporations have a very strict policy on gifts. At General Mills in Minneapolis, for example, employees are not allowed to accept any gifts of money and any present they receive cannot be worth more than $25. Many other large companies don't allow their employees to accept gifts at all.
INTERVIEWER:	I see. But what should you do if your company does not have an official policy on accepting gifts? Is it best to keep quiet or should you tell other people about them?
KELLY:	Well, if you're in doubt, I suggest discussing it with a colleague or supervisor and seeing what they feel about it. You see, if it's out in the open, no one can accuse you later of accepting a bribe.
INTERVIEWER:	Uh uh. And what should you do if you don't want to accept a gift from a business partner? I mean, you don't want to offend someone by refusing their gift. What do you suggest here?
KELLY:	Well, one solution is to donate the gift to charity. Obviously if you do something like this, it's only polite to write a note explaining what you've done …

14.3 B

I remember the first time I was in Spain on business. I was at a meeting and it was going really well, the language was no problem, we were racing through the agenda and I was thinking this is great, I'll be able to fly home late tonight with a deal in my briefcase. And then my stomach started rumbling!

Well, I looked at my watch. It was one thirty. These people must eat something soon, I thought. Two thirty. I was getting desperate. Quarter to three. Do they really survive on nothing but black coffee and cigarettes, I asked myself.

Half an hour later one of my business partners got up to phone and check that there was a table at his favourite Basque restaurant just around the corner.

Finally, at three thirty, I had a small glass of lager and some olives in front of me and a menu in my hand. We then went on to have this amazing three-hour lunch, during which we concluded our deal, and I was actually able to get an earlier flight.

But I learnt my lesson. Now, when I go to Spain, I make sure I have a second breakfast around eleven so I can survive until mid-afternoon without having to eat my fingernails. And now I know why I can never reach my business contacts between eleven and twelve – they're all out for a second breakfast!

15

MAN 1:	You've been to Kuala Lumpur, Mark. Tell me, what's the best way into town from the airport?
MAN 2:	Well, you can take a taxi or go by bus. A taxi'll cost you about 25 Ringgits. A bus is cheaper at 7 Ringgits. But they'll both get you there!
MAN 1:	Uh uh. And what about getting around downtown?
MAN 2:	I always take a taxi. They're really cheap. Most fares within the central downtown area are less than 5 Ringgits, although you pay an extra Ringgit for a taxi from a hotel, and an additional 50 per cent between midnight and 6 a.m.
MAN 1:	Do you have to negotiate the fare, or what?
MAN 2:	Not usually. Taxis are metered. Just make sure the meter is turned on! The only problem is during the rush hour or when it rains. If you actually manage to find a taxi, the driver often refuses to go to a congested area, but if you offer twice or three times the going rate, he'll usually change his mind! The way to avoid messing around is to negotiate an hourly rate to hire a taxi for 20 to 25 Ringgits. By the way, not all drivers speak good English.
MAN 1:	What's public transport like?
MAN 2:	Not bad. Some of the city buses and minibuses are air-conditioned and quite respectable. And they're very cheap. Minibuses cost 60 sen for any distance, ordinary buses start at 20 sen and increase with distance.
MAN 1:	And car hire?
MAN 2:	That's no problem. That costs about 150 Ringgits a day. And petrol is cheap. Last time I was there it was just 1 Ringgit a litre. However, I personally don't think it's worth driving yourself, taxis are inexpensive and parking is often difficult.

16.3 C

PRESENTER:	Women have been the job market's big success story in the past twenty years. But as they have found jobs, men have lost them. This week we ask whether women have driven men from the workplace. Over to Ms Holmes.
HOLMES:	In the past two decades, every country in the Organization for Economic Cooperation and Development has seen a rise in the number of women who enter the workforce. At the same time, the number of men in work has fallen. There are two reasons for this. Firstly, younger men have stayed in education longer; secondly, older men have been taking earlier retirement. As a result, in America, for example, 46 per cent of the workforce are now women. And if things continue like this, the typical worker in some rich countries will be a woman by the 21st century.
PRESENTER:	Why are more women going out to work nowadays?
HOLMES:	Most of the increase is a result of the way married women arrange their lives; in the past, most women stayed at home to look after their children; now they return to work as soon as their youngest child is at school – or often sooner.
PRESENTER:	But is it easier for women to find jobs than for men?
HOLMES:	Yes, but this is because in all rich countries, most women do just a handful of jobs, they're secretaries, shop assistants, cashiers, nurses, kitchen hands, nannies and so on.
PRESENTER:	So women are not taking men's jobs.
HOLMES:	No, not at all. But what has happened is that 'women's' jobs have expanded while traditional 'male' jobs have been disappearing. For example, women are less likely than men to work in manufacturing. So as manufacturing jobs have disappeared, it's mostly men who have been thrown out of work. On the other hand, employment in service industries has increased. And women have benefited from this …

17.1 B

MAN:	I'm drafting some proposals for greening the office and I'd like your opinion, Maria. Have you got a minute?
WOMAN:	Yes, sure. Go ahead.
MAN:	Right, here's the first proposal. We should write to our customers on recycled paper. What are your views on that, Maria?
WOMAN:	Hmm. I'm afraid I don't think that's a very good idea. I mean, I don't think our customers would like that at all.
MAN:	OK. Next one, then. What do you think about using china cups instead of plastic ones for the drinks machine?
WOMAN:	Sorry, I'm afraid I don't think that's a very good idea either. I mean, where are we going to wash them, we haven't got a kitchen, we'd have to get one.
MAN:	True. Well, try this one. We should encourage the staff to cycle to work. How do you feel about that?
WOMAN:	Oh dear, I'm sorry to be so negative, but I'm afraid I don't think that's a very good idea either. Even if people bring their work clothes to the office, there's nowhere for them to shower or change. And you can't have people running around the office in jogging suits all day. What would our visitors think?
MAN:	Hmm. OK. Now, fourth proposal. I suggest banning smoking on company premises. What do you think about that?
WOMAN:	Yeah, that's more like it. I agree with you on that. It would actually be quite good for our image being in the health care business.
MAN:	Good, I'm glad you agree on something! Next one, er, we should start sorting the rubbish in the

	offices. You know, have separate bins for paper, plastics and that sort of thing.
WOMAN:	Yeah, that's a good idea, too. We could collect the paper for recycling, er, as long as we don't have to write to customers on it afterwards!
MAN:	OK. Now, last one. How do you feel about using refillable pens instead of biros in the office, Maria?
WOMAN:	Yes, that's a good idea. I agree with you on that, too.

17.2 B

CHAIR:	Right. Let's move on to the next point, er, that's the packaging of *Black Musk*. Would you like to start, James?
JAMES:	Well, I think we should stick to plastic bottles. It's worked well with all our other products. And the advantages outweigh the disadvantages. I mean, plastic bottles are light, they're easy to pack, they're easy to transport. And what's really important, there's no problem with breakages.
CHAIR:	Olivia, what are your views?
OLIVIA:	I'm afraid I don't agree with you, James. This bath oil is going to be more expensive than others in our range and I think it's important to go for a more upmarket image. I think we should use glass.
CHAIR:	Right. What do you think, Max?
MAX:	I agree.
JAMES:	Sorry, with who?
MAX:	With Olivia. What's more, we ought to reconsider the whole question of recycling. If we're going to encourage customers to bring back their containers, glass will be easier to clean than plastic.
JAMES:	But do you really think people will bring back their containers for refills?
CHAIR:	Laura?
LAURA:	Can I just say something? Has anyone thought about the question of suppliers? I mean, if we use glass, we'll have to find a new supplier. Our present supplier doesn't do glass as far as I know.
JAMES:	Good point. So perhaps we should stick to plastic.
CHAIR:	Well, perhaps someone could get some quotes?
LAURA:	Yes, OK. I can do that.
CHAIR:	Right. So OK. Now let's move on to the next point …

18.1 B

MAN:	So when did you actually introduce flexitime?
WOMAN:	About a year ago.
MAN:	And has it been successful?
WOMAN:	I think so. After a few teething problems. You know, people forgetting to clock off when they went home and things like that.
MAN:	So could you tell me how your system works?
WOMAN:	Well, everyone has to work a certain number of hours a month, at the moment it's 140. Within limits, we can choose when we work, for example we can start as early as seven in the morning and work as late as seven at night.
MAN:	But you must have some kind of core time when people have to be at their place of work? Otherwise there'd be absolute chaos.
WOMAN:	That's right. Our core time's between nine and twelve in the morning and two and four in the afternoon.
MAN:	What happens about breaks? Coffee breaks and lunch breaks? Do you clock off for them?

WOMAN:	Well, we don't have to clock off for coffee breaks, we usually just go and get a coffee when we need it, but we do have to clock off for lunch.
MAN:	And what about overtime? I mean, what happens if someone works more than 140 hours in a month?
WOMAN:	Well, overtime's no longer paid, but we can take free time instead, up to two days each month. That's quite useful, really. For doctor's appointments and things like that.
MAN:	Have you introduced flexitime throughout the company?
WOMAN:	At the moment, it's just in Administration. In Production they're still working two shifts a day, but they are thinking of introducing some form of flexible working time. A flexible week or something like that, but you should talk to the Production Manager about that. He'll be able to tell you more about it …

18.3 A

Good morning everyone and welcome to Hershey!

I'm going to tell you something about the history of the Hershey company before we go off and find out how chocolate is really made.

Let's start by going back over a hundred years in time. Did you know that chocolate was a real luxury then? Something that only rich people could afford to buy? So how come we all eat it today? We have Milton S. Hershey, the founder of Hershey to thank for that. He had a dream. And his dream was to make good chocolate that didn't cost a lot of money.

Now, one of Mr Hershey's first businesses was the Lancaster Caramel Company. This business was founded in 1886 and was very successful. But when Mr Hershey saw some German chocolate manufacturing machinery at the World's Columbian Exposition in Chicago in 1893, he decided he wanted to make chocolate himself.

In 1900, Mr Hershey sold the Lancaster Caramel Company for $1 million. He used the money from this sale to build what is now the world's largest chocolate manufacturing plant. The completion of the Hershey chocolate factory in 1905 meant the mass production of chocolate could begin.

Mr Hershey's chocolate business flourished and so did the community around it. A bank, a department store, a school and even a zoo were built in rapid succession and in 1906 the village of Derry Church was renamed Hershey after its founder, Milton S. Hershey.

Many of Hershey's major products date back to these early years. *Hershey's Kisses*, for example, were first manufactured in 1907 and the *Mr Goodbar* chocolate bar was introduced in 1925. Then in 1927 the Hershey Chocolate Company was renamed the Hershey Chocolate Corporation and listed on the New York Stock Exchange for the first time …

19.2 C

Message one

This is Shena. I've just got your message asking about the catering arrangements at the conference. Er, there'll be a buffet midday and in the evening with a variety of both meat and non-meat dishes, so I don't think there'll be problems for vegetarians.

Message two

Hello. Rohinton speaking. I'm returning your call about expenses for the sales conference. Er, tell participants that we pay for hotel accommodation and transfers from the airport, but they're expected to pay for their flights. Actually, if you can get them to let you know when they're arriving, you might be able to arrange for some of them to share taxis from the airport.

20

One

INTERVIEWER: How long does it take to produce a car in Japan?
MAN 1: About 16.8 hours.
INTERVIEWER: And what about quality? How many defects are there per 100 cars?
MAN 1: On average, 60, although we're trying to reduce this figure.
INTERVIEWER: Could you tell me something about the way you organize your workforce?
MAN 1: Teamwork is very important to us; we try to do as much as possible in teams. At present I'd say about 70 per cent of the workforce are organized into teams. I think one of the benefits of this is that our workers also make a lot of suggestions for improvement. We get an average of 62 suggestions per worker per year.
INTERVIEWER: How many different job classifications do you have in the factory?
MAN 1: Twelve.
INTERVIEWER: And what about training? How much time do you spend training new workers?
MAN 1: Training is very important. We spend an average of about 380 hours training a new worker.
INTERVIEWER: What percentage of the production process is automated?
MAN 1: The welding process is most fully automated. About 86 per cent of that is done by robots. Just over half – er 55 per cent, to be exact - of the painting process and just 2 per cent of the assembly process is automated. It's still early days, but we're hoping to automate up to 50 per cent of the final assembly process as, on the one hand, it's difficult for us to find young people who are prepared to work in factories and, on the other hand, we think automation makes factories nicer places to work in. However, it's not only the most labour-intensive part of the factory, but also the trickiest to automate.

Two

INTERVIEWER: How long does it take to produce a car in Europe?
MAN 2: At present, an average of 36.2 hours.
INTERVIEWER: And what about quality? How many defects are there per 100 cars?
MAN 2: We reckon on about 97.
INTERVIEWER: Could you tell me something about the way you organize your workforce?
MAN 2: Teamwork is not a big issue here in Europe. At the moment, only about 0.6 per cent of the workforce are organized into teams. This shows in that we don't get many suggestions for improvement from our workers; it works out at something like 0.4 per employee per year.
INTERVIEWER: How many different job classifications do you have in the factory?
MAN 2: Fifteen.
INTERVIEWER: And what about training? How much time do you spend training new workers?
MAN 2: Quite a lot, on average it works out at 197 hours per new employee.
INTERVIEWER: What percentage of the production process is automated?
MAN 2: About 77 per cent of the welding process, 38 per cent of the painting and 3 per cent of the assembly process at the moment.

Thanks and acknowledgements

The authors would like to thank their colleagues at Insearch Language Centre, University of Technology, Sydney, Australia, and at International House, Freiburg, Germany, especially Dieter Löffner, and also Sue Unwin-Späth and Peter Späth of Freiburg, Germany.

The authors and publishers are grateful to the following copyright holders for permission to reproduce copyright material. Every endeavour has been made to contact the copyright holders and apologies are expressed for any omissions.

p. 8: MasterCard reproduced with the kind permission of MasterCard International Incorporated. pp. 8 and 62: American Express card reproduced by kind permission of American Express. p. 12: 'Instant office at the ready' from *Asiaweek* 28 April 1993. pp. 19, 91 and 98: Dilbert cartoons reproduced with permission of Knight Features. pp. 21 and 73: The Far Side by Gary Larson. p. 21 © 1988 Farworks, Inc. p. 73 © 1987 Farworks, Inc. Used with permission. All Rights Reserved p. 29: Photograph by Craig Easton reproduced by permission of *The Independent*. 'Another million made, then back in time for school' by Geoffrey Beattie from *The Independent on Sunday*, 21 May 1995. pp. 42, 43, 89, 92, 102, 113, 118, 119 and 123: From *The Economist*, pp. 42 and 43 from 16 September 1995 issue, p. 89 from 27 February 1993, pp. 92 and 118 from 5 March 1994, p. 102 from 17 October 1992, p. 113 from 17 October 1992, pp. 119 and 123 from 28 October 1995. p. 50: reproduced with kind permission of First Direct. p. 57: 'The itch to switch' by Naomi Caine from *The Sunday Times*, 25 February 1996. © Times Newspapers Limited, 1996. p. 60: logos used here are trade marks of the British Broadcasting Corporation and are used under licence. p. 61: materials for this photo collage kindly supplied by Kwik-Fit. p. 62: logo reproduced with the permission of Levi Strauss and Company. p. 62: extract from the *Conqueror Small Business Handbook* reproduced with permission from Arjo Wiggins Fine Papers Limited. p. 66: Text and graphs from 1992 Annual Report and photograph reproduced courtesy of Volvo. p. 74: cartoon by Dean Vietor © 1977 from The New Yorker Collection. All Rights Reserved. p. 75: 'How to collect money on time' reproduced with permission of Barclays Bank Plc. p. 91: 'What are your personal standards?' first appeared in Working Woman February 1990. Reprinted with permission of MacDonald Communications Corporation. Copyright 1997 by MacDonald Communications Corporation. For subscriptions e-mail at GMPMCC@aol.com. pp. 104 and 105: text and illustrations reproduced by kind permission of Hershey Foods Corporation, Hershey, PA, USA. p. 110: text and photographs used by kind permission of KEF Audio (UK) Limited. p. 113: 'Japanese standards? No problem' © Telegraph Group Ltd. London 1996.

The authors and publishers are grateful to the following illustrators and photographic sources:

Illustrators:
Gerry Ball: pp. 4, 26, 52; Kathy Baxendale: pp. 33, 34, 40, 41, 57, 64, 92, 102, 106, 118, 119, 121, 123, 124; Peter Byatt: pp. 7, 32, 54, 63; David Downton; pp. 10 *b*, 18, 24 *t*, 77, 81, 90, 95, 111; Annie Farrall: p. 65; Edward McLachlan: pp. 53, 103, 116, 120; Giovanna Pierce: p. 6; Tracy Rich: pp. 10 *t*, 24 *b*, 25, 35, 38, 44, 68.

Photographers / Photographic sources:
Ace Photo Agency: pp. 71/Michael Bluestone, 39 *bl*/ Ronald Toms; Anthony Blake PhotoLibrary/Gerrit Buntrock: p. 82; Arosa Kulm Hotel, Arosa, Switzerland, p. 107 *l*; Britstock-IFA: pp. 93 *tm*/Steve Altman, 93 *tl*/ Roger Cracknell, 101/1PL; Cambridge University Press: pp. 67, 85; Will Capel: pp. 23, 80 *tl* & *bl*; Colorific/David White/Black Star: p. 39 *br*; Comstock Inc., pp. 32, 34 *l*, 52 *l*; James Davis Travel Photography: pp. 22 *mr* & *bl*; Maggie Murray/Format: p. 93 *bl*; Getty Images: pp. 39 *t*/Don Bonsey, 100 *m*/Tim Brown, 47/Lonnie Duke, 94 *bl*/Ed Pritchard; Robert Harding Picture Library/Gavin Hellier: p. 80 *r*; David Hoffman: p. 94 *mr*; The Image Bank: pp. 30, 42, 43/Gary Craile, 5/L.D. Gordon, 51 *r*/Romily Lockyer; Chris Moyse/Impact Photos: p. 72 *br*; Life File/Jeremy Hoare: pp. 66 & 69; John Sturrock/Network: p. 100 *r*, Anthony Suau/Network: p. 100 *l*; Christine Osborne Pictures: pp. 22 *br*, 72 *mr*; Ross Parry Picture Agency, p. 88 *b*; Le Montreux Palace, Montreux, Switzerland, p. 107 *r*, 108 *bl* and *r*; Jeremy Pembrey: pp. 17, 49, 61, 74, 78, 94 *br*, 97; Pictor International: pp. 15 *t*, 16, 20, 72 *bl*; Pictures Colour Library: p. 40; PowerStock Photo Library: pp. 10, 15 *b*, 96; Spectrum Colour Library: p. 22 *ml*; SuperStock Ltd., pp. 4, 9, 34 *r*; Jan Anderson/Sygma: pp. 88 *t*, 93 *r*; Telegraph Colour Library: pp. 22 *t*, 25, 44 *t* & 48/Benelux Press, 94 *tr* & 99/V.C.L.; Trip Photographic Agency: pp. 12/R Brown, 33/M. Mackenzie.

(*l* = left, *r* = right, *t* = top, *b* = bottom, *m* = middle)

Edited by James Dale.
Design and composition by Newton Harris.
Picture research by Sandie Huskinson-Rolfe of PHOTOSEEKERS.
Audio cassette produced by James Richardson at Studio AVP, London.